ARE
PAROCHIAL
SCHOOLS
THE ANSWER?

Mary Perkins Ryan

ARE
PAROCHIAL
SCHOOLS
THE ANSWER?

CATHOLIC
EDUCATION
IN THE
LIGHT OF
THE COUNCIL

Holt, Rinehart and Winston   New York   Chicago   San Francisco

FOREWORD

AMERICAN Catholic education, as a system, is in a state of crisis. Logistics—the continuous and ever increasing demand for personnel and financial resources—have forced the leadership of the Church in the United States to rethink the whole question of the educational system and to reassay its value in the light of the modern religious climate.

In a dispassionate and exhaustive study, Mary Perkins Ryan, moved by the spirit of free and open discussion fostered by the Second Vatican Council, brings much light and no heat to this vexing problem.

Catholic education has but one purpose—the formation of a people acceptable to God. And the people will become acceptable to God when they know, love, and serve Him and know, love, and serve one another in Him. This is the Church, Christ and His people—a living organism, working in history, growing, developing. It is, then, by nature dynamic, not static. If there is to be progress, there must be change. Means that were useful and necessary in one age must give way to others in a new and different age.

With this in mind and with Pope John's call for *aggiornamento* in her ears, the author asks some very pertinent questions. For the formation of God's

v

people, given the modern religious climate of the United States, is the Catholic educational system, as we know it, necessary or even desirable? Are we still prisoners of a seige mentality: negative, defensive, fearful of threats from without? Must we continue to make the school the central and normal means of Christian formation? Should we move the focus from the classroom to the home, the Church, and the public forum where Christianity is lived? Do we need information or guidance? Can we afford to spend almost all of our resources—personnel, money, and effort—on an educational system that is fast becoming contained, that is reaching a smaller and smaller proportion of our people at the expense of the religious formation of all Catholics and of the great missionary vocation and responsibility of the Church? Can the American Church continue to give a general education to an elite, leaving its children in the public schools, in the secular and state universities, and in adult life without adequate religious formation?

The history of the Church shows that, for the most part, her people obtained their religious formation from the scriptures, the liturgy, and the sacraments, lived in their daily lives. Can a return to such a formation disestablish the Catholic school system?

This is an interesting, well-written, informative, and provocative work. Not a few will disagree with Mrs. Ryan's thesis. Few may be convinced by her arguments. But certainly she has opened a window—and perhaps a door—on this crucial subject by her frank and intelligent discussion.

✠ ERNEST J. PRIMEAU, S.T.D.
BISHOP OF MANCHESTER, N.H.

PREFACE

All those who have been following the current debate on the problems of religious schools and of religion in schools are concerned that a solution be found which will do justice at once to the claims of religion and to those of our pluralistic society. But an increasing number, of whom the writer is one, are beginning to think that these problems are being discussed in too narrow a context.

Some time ago, before the prospect of vastly increased Federal aid to education and the discussion of public school prayers and of related cases raised the issue afresh, I began to wonder whether the whole question of religious education should not be examined from a viewpoint wider than the usual one. I had been studying various aspects of religious education for many years, and had also experienced the difficulties parents face in trying to give their children a religious formation and to continue their own. As a result, I came more and more to believe, on the one hand, that the parochial school system does not and cannot answer present needs, and on the other hand, that recent trends in the Catholic Church, culminating in the Second Vatican Council, are indicating both the form which the question of religious education should take and the way in which it should be answered.

When I proposed—first to close friends and eventually to priests, religious, and lay people in many parts of the country—this idea which to me seemed so revolutionary, I discovered that the majority had already come to much the same conclusions, and were eager to help me deepen and clarify my ideas. The present book is thus the fruit of considerable thinking, not only on my own part but on that of others, to whom I should like here to express my gratitude for their invaluable and continued assistance.

Although this book is specifically concerned with the problems of the Roman Catholic Church in regard to religious formation, I hope that it may also prove useful to those of other faiths. How is a people "acceptable to God" to be formed? This is the basic issue underlying both Jewish and Christian problems of religious education. If we can all see it and discuss it in a context wider than that of schools and formal education, we may be on the way to finding a truly religious and a truly American answer—and so to solving one of the thorniest problems facing both organized religion and democracy today.

MARY PERKINS RYAN

August 1963
Goffstown, N.H.

CONTENTS

Foreword   v
Preface   vii

1   The Present Situation   3
2   Hints From History   20
3   It All Goes Together   46
4   Who Needs Formation?   72
5   New Vistas   93
6   Fears—Realistic and Otherwise   114
7   The Initial Effort   127
8   With or Without a Catholic School System?   137
9   New Resources for the Church   161
10   A New Climate in the Church   166
11   Conclusions   171

ARE
PAROCHIAL
SCHOOLS
THE ANSWER?

1

THE
PRESENT
SITUATION

SPEAKING with a group of priests in the spring of 1963, a bishop remarked that it would be many years before the effects of the Second Vatican Council would show themselves. One of the priests answered: "It has already had an effect, or Your Excellency would not be speaking to so many non-Catholic audiences."

The ecumenical spirit of the Council, its pastoral orientation, the fact that it was called to bring about an *aggiornamento,* a "todaying" of the Church, and that the majority of the Council Fathers have shown themselves eager that it should do so—all of these have had their effect quite apart from specific measures. They have created a climate and have also indicated the ultimate direction of the Council's work. It is particularly significant that the first fruit of that work has been agreement upon principles for reform in two major interconnected areas—the sacramental rites and the way in which the faith is to be presented.[1] For there could be no clearer indication of

[1] These principles, set out in the preface and first part of the Constitution on the Sacred Liturgy, were summarized by Fr. Cypriano Vagaggini in *L'Osservatore Romano* (December 8, 1962). A

3

how deeply the renewal is to permeate Catholic life, or of one of the major ways in which it is to do so.

The general outlook of the Council is, then, sufficiently clear for us to begin to re-evaluate our present institutions and ways of doing things. A consensus of the majority of theologians is ordinarily taken as expressing the mind of the Church at a given time on a given topic. Certainly, then, the consensus of the majority of the bishops of the world, the supreme teachers of Christ's flock, as set forth in the debates at the first session[2] as well as in the voting on the Constitution on the Liturgy, may be taken as expressing the mind of the Church as to the main lines of the *aggiornamento*.

It is particularly urgent that we begin immediately to make an assessment of the Catholic school system in the light of the Council, since all educational planning obviously must take future trends into consideration. The urgency is all the greater since many spokesmen for the Church, and likewise many parents —with lawyers to support them and politicians to press their claims—are busy doing all they can to prove to the American public that public aid for schools conducted under religious auspices is both reasonable and constitutional. And if surveys are a

translation of his article, under the title "The Important Chapter One," was published in *Worship*, February, 1963. The constitution as a whole was approved almost unanimously at the second session and promulgated by Pope Paul VI on December 4, 1963.

[2] The subjects discussed were the Liturgy, the Sources of Revelation, Communications media, Unity, and the Church. See Xavier Rynne, *Letters from Vatican City* (New York: Farrar, Straus & Co., 1963).

reliable indication, they are winning more and more adherents to their position.

As everyone knows, the Catholic school system must gain public support if it is to be extended or even maintained. Because of rising costs, an expanding school population, the shortage of teachers, and the raising of standards for teachers, as well as for buildings and equipment, it will soon be practically impossible for unaided Catholic efforts to continue to handle the proportion of Catholic young people now being served. And for the original goal of "every Catholic child in a Catholic school," from kindergarten through graduate school, there is clearly no hope at all.

If we must have our own schools in order to form young people as Catholics, it is obvious that we must continue and extend the present effort to seek public aid. But if the outlook and directives of the Council indicate the need for a new approach to the problem of religious formation[3]—if it seems likely that in five, ten, or twenty-five years a Catholic school system will be neither as necessary nor as desirable as it has been in the past—then much of our current effort is misdirected, quite apart from the considerable ill will it is producing toward the Church. If there is even a possibility that such waste of effort and slowing down of ecumenical progress might be prevented, surely that possibility should be seriously examined. Moreover, such an examination might prove to be the first

[3] This term is used as being more comprehensive than "instruction" and as synonymous with "education" in the very broad sense of the development and training of the whole person—here, the whole *Christian* person.

step toward planning and beginning to put into effect a religious formation that would implement the *aggiornamento*.

The notion prevails, among Catholics and non-Catholics alike, that elementary schools, high schools, and colleges under Catholic auspices are an essential aspect of Catholic life, and that belief in the necessity of a Catholic educational system is almost an article of Catholic faith. But, in actual fact, providing a general education for its children is an auxiliary service, not part of the essential mission of the Church. Whether such a service is required for the welfare of the Church in a given era is a question of policy, not of faith. In the last century, at a time when the establishment of parochial schools was about to be made a matter of Church law, there was serious debate as to the wisdom of this policy; clearly, then, it is not heresy to reopen the discussion today. On the contrary, a serious review of the fundamentals of this question seems a vital necessity for the future welfare of the American Church.

To initiate such a discussion is the aim of this book. It will begin with a brief outline of the present situation in order to see where we stand, followed by a survey of the major solutions of the Church to the problem of religious formation in the past, so as to locate our present solution in its historical context. Next will be an attempt to analyze the mentality of the recent American past which made a Catholic school system seem the only possible solution and brought about our present concentration of effort on children. It will then be time to consider whether

6

this concentration is really effective—whether it would be more realistic, even for the sake of our children, to plan our educational efforts to reach the whole Catholic community, in accord with the new mentality now taking shape in the Church and diffused by the Council. Some current fears concerning possible effects of the new mentality will then be examined, as the prelude to an outline of the effort that will be required to communicate it to the whole Catholic body in this country.

All this will necessitate some discussion of the basic aims of religious education according to the old mentality and the new, and therefore of the basic aims of the Catholic religion itself and of the lives of those who adhere to it. It is no news to those who have followed the Council's work that although Catholic truth is itself unchanging, the way in which Catholics look at this truth does change; and, obviously, it makes a vast difference in practical policy what point of view the Church adopts in a given age. The reader who is mainly concerned with questions of school policy is therefore asked to bear with this discussion of religious issues, since it is only in the light of those issues that such practical questions can be satisfactorily solved.

Only at this point, and not before, shall we be in a position to inquire dispassionately whether or not a Catholic school system is ultimately either essential or desirable in attaining the objectives of the Council. Although the final chapter presents my own conclusions, the book does not pretend to be the last word on the subject; it is intended, as I said above, simply to serve as a preface and a stimulant to widespread open discussion of all issues involved—the real issues facing Catholic education today.

As everyone knows, Catholic education in this country is an enormous enterprise. A survey conducted by the magazine *Catholic Building and Maintenance* showed that in 1960 almost $100,000,000 was to be spent on parochial-school maintenance, operation, and renovation, and that in 1958 alone, $175,-000,000 had been spent on new elementary- and high-school construction. It concluded that the cost of duplicating the present system of Catholic school facilities would be more than seven billion dollars, and that if the taxpayers in local communities were obliged to maintain and operate the parochial schools now in existence, they would have to put out an additional 1.8 billion dollars annually.

According to figures taken from the general summary in the Official Catholic Directory for 1963, in that year an estimated 4,524,393 children would be attending 10,322 parochial elementary and institutional schools and an additional 84,636 would be in private Catholic elementary schools under a total of 111,091 teachers; 623,897 other young people would be attending 1,537 diocesan and parochial high schools and an additional 381,048 would be attending 895 private Catholic high schools, all these staffed by 46,625 teachers; and there would be 300,000 students at 282 Catholic colleges and universities with faculties totaling over 25,000. A complete picture would also have to include all the brothers, sisters, and priests destined for teaching and still in training,

8

along with those training them, and all retired religious teachers and those caring for them. It would also include the pastors responsible for schools and the staffs of the various diocesan and national organizations and of publications devoted to Catholic education.

All this, of course, has been accomplished with no state support other than that provided by the tax-free status of educational institutions and by the fringe benefits allowed in some places—such as bus rides and hot lunches. As an achievement, therefore, the Catholic educational system certainly witnesses to the zeal and determination of American Catholics. It is no wonder that it is the pride of the American Church, pointed to and praised by bishops from other lands and by visiting dignitaries from Rome.

But, despite all this effort, the proportion of Catholic young people reached by Catholic education is estimated to be only about 55 per cent on the elementary level, 45 per cent on the high-school level and 37 per cent on the college level,[4] and everything

---

[4] More accurate figures are expected to be compiled from the data gathered in the Carnegie Study of Catholic Education. Some authorities believe the present estimates to be somewhat high both because they are not completely up to date and because they are based on school registration figures compared with parish census figures. If the school figures were compared with baptismal register figures for the entire country (necessitated by mobility), it seems likely that a far lower figure of Catholic school attendance in proportion to the total would be the result. Again, on the basis of the above estimates, the total Catholic elementary-school population would be 8,380,472 and the total Catholic high-school population only 2,233,171, whereas one would expect it to be something nearer half of the elementary-school figure. Even allowing for the

points to a decrease in these percentages unless public support is obtained.

Yet, although it reaches only a part of the Catholic school and college population, the Catholic educational system involves a large proportion of the Church's available manpower, resources, and zeal. Quite aside from the vast amount of episcopal and pastoral time and attention required for administrative tasks, or the enormous lay effort expended to support our educational institutions, out of the 59,-581 priests in the country, some 12,840 are taken up with the work of education, and some 5,281 Brothers out of 11,502, and some 103,141 Sisters out of 173,351, are likewise engaged.[5]

By comparison, the number of priests and religious[6]

fact that many high-school students drop out as soon as they can legally do so, it would appear that the proportion of Catholic students attending Catholic high schools must be considerably lower than 45 per cent of the total.

[5] The educational figures are from the National Catholic Welfare Conference report on education for 1961, the general figures from the Catholic Directory Supplement of 1962. The number of priests given here does not include the more than 3,000 teaching in seminaries and religious houses of formation or the 2,203 who are part-time teachers of religion in Catholic schools.

[6] The term "religious" has so many different connotations as to need explanation. It comes from a Latin word meaning "to bind"; thus "religion" is what binds man to God, and a religious person, in the usual sense of the term, is one who lives in the consciousness of his relation to God. But a "religious" is a man or woman who has bound himself or herself by vows to live according to a particular rule of life approved by the Church, a rule designed to bring him or her into a continually more intimate relation with God. By a "religious teacher," here is meant a teacher who is a "religious" in this sense, not someone engaged in giving religious instruction.

—not to speak of effort and money—concerned with the work of providing *religious* instruction for the millions of young people not in Catholic schools and colleges is almost negligible. Figures on the work of religious instruction of young people not in Catholic schools, made up from reports sent in by directors of the Confraternity of Christian Doctrine from 81 of the 133 dioceses in the United States, report 28,718 active religious teachers and 35,521 active lay teachers, reaching 1,226,428 elementary school children through weekly classes during the school year, 566,-562 in vacation schools, and 379,464 high school students. These figures do not include any mention of the religious instruction being carried out in the other dioceses and outside the framework of the Confraternity. The Catholic Directory Summary for 1963 reports released-time classes as enrolling a total of 909,424 elementary-school children and 1,119,800 high-school students, but does not give the number of teachers engaged in this work.[7] In any case, it seems clear that a very considerable number of Catholic young people are not being reached at all.

On the high-school level the situation is particularly depressing. Everyone agrees that the adolescent period is crucial—that a person's whole way of looking at life for the future is usually determined during these years. Adequate religious formation is possibly

---

[7] If all the figures were available, it would be interesting to compare the number of teacher hours per week during the school year devoted throughout the United States to the religious instruction of Catholic elementary and high school students outside of Catholic schools with the number of teacher-hours devoted to general subjects in Catholic elementary and high schools.

more essential here than at any other period of youth. And yet nobody seems to have found practical answers to the question of how to provide young people of this age not in Catholic schools with an adequate religious formation. While various texts for it are being composed and used experimentally, there is no general agreement on what this formation could or should consist in. Few people in authority seem to be aware of the importance and magnitude of the problem. What makes a solution even more difficult to find is that many parents think of religious education as something only for younger children, with the result that too often they do not see to it that their teen-agers attend classes when these are provided.

Again, there are some 500,000 Catholic students on secular campuses (as against 300,000 in Catholic colleges and universities), but for all these students there are only 140 full-time chaplains, some of whom divide their time between three and four campuses (whereas at Notre Dame, for instance, 89 priests and Brothers care for 6,700 students). Only about 50,000 members are reported by the 547 nationally affiliated Newman Clubs, though an additional 325 nonaffiliated clubs have not reported their membership.

It would seem, then, that there exists a great disproportion between the effort spent on the young people who attend Catholic schools and colleges and on those who do not. This disproportion is often defended by the argument that the best we can do is to give a thoroughly Catholic formation to a part of our Catholic young people, who will then—it is hoped —act as a leaven to the rest.

But there remains the all-important question of

whether or not such a formation is actually being given in Catholic schools and colleges—a question that does not appear to have engaged the attention of the great majority of those responsible for the Catholic educational system. But while they seem to take it for granted that all is well, an increasing number of Catholic parents, teachers, and priests are beginning to wonder. How far does what is being done actually correspond, they are asking, with the specifications laid down by Pius XI in his encyclical, *The Christian Education of Youth?*

The proper and immediate end of Christian education is to cooperate with divine grace in forming the true and perfect Christian, that is, to form Christ Himself in those regenerated by baptism. . . . The mere fact that a school gives some religious instruction . . . does not bring it into accord with the rights of the Church and the Christian family, or make it a fit place for Catholic students. To be this, it is necessary that all its teaching and the whole organization of the school, and its teachers, syllabi, and textbooks in every branch, be regulated by the Christian spirit, . . . so that religion may be in very truth the foundation and crown of the youth's entire training.

From the older, conventional point of view, the point of view still widely held today, our Catholic schools seem to be meeting these requirements of Pius XI by giving religious instruction and general education in a religious atmosphere. But from the point of view of the catechetical renewal which has slowly been gaining ground over the last decades, it appears certain that the whole question of the objectives, the content, and the manner of religious instruction needs to be thought out afresh.

True, it was realized some time ago that methods of teaching religion should be improved. A multitude of "catechetical aids"—pictures, coloring books, diagrams, questions breaking up the catechism answers, and so on—have been worked out to help adapt the truths of the faith as set down in the catechism to the learning requirements of each age level. But the matter of this religious instruction is still, generally speaking, the questions and answers of the Baltimore Catechism, and the aim is still merely to fix the answers firmly in the children's memories.

The revolution in religious teaching is already under way. Unfortunately, many think of the "new catechetics" as merely another method; they do not realize the radical change in approach, necessitating a new mentality on the part of the teacher, as well as new textbooks and learning aids. The term "catechetics," in fact, has been brought back into use precisely to show that it is something quite different from "religious instruction" as this is still commonly conceived today. The word "catechism" is familiar to everyone as meaning a book containing questions and answers; but the Greek root means "to cause to resound" and so "to instruct, to inform." The term "catechetics," signifying the art and science of religious instruction, is meant to have the same connotations as the "catechesis" given in the early Church and newly brought out in the Constitution on the Sacred Liturgy accepted by the Council: a presentation centered on sacred history and on Christ as the center of that history, with its sources in Scripture and the liturgy, and having as its aim the personal involvement of the Christian in Christ's work of salvation.[8]

The problems involved in "forming the true and perfect Christian, forming Christ Himself" in young people, are so serious that they ought, surely, to be engaging the best minds and the major efforts in every institution and in all of our educational organizations. Those chosen to teach religion in high schools and colleges ought to be the cream of the teaching staff. In elementary schools, where one teacher handles many subjects, each teacher ought to to have had at least as much training in how to teach religion as in how to teach, say, arithmetic or geography.

Some institutions and individuals are in fact beginning to give this all-important question the attention it deserves. But many of those in authority still hopefully believe that what is being done is all that either can or need be done. On the other hand, what is being done seems increasingly unsatisfactory to more and more Catholics. Many parents are asking themselves: Must we sacrifice so much in order to get our children into Catholic schools, only to watch them receiving an inadequate religious training? Some, indeed, have gone so far as to take their chil-

[8] See Gerard S. Sloyan, ed., *Modern Catechetics: Message and Method in Religious Formation* (New York: The Macmillan Company, 1963); also Shawn Sheehan, "Council's Decrees on Liturgy Open New Vistas," *Mediator,* December, 1962.

dren out of Catholic schools because they feel that they can give them a better Catholic formation at home.

Unfortunately, it is all too probable that the current revolution in arithmetic will reach Catholic schools long before the revolution in teaching religion. Catholic educators are easily convinced that they should study the latest methods of teaching mathematics; the subject not being a Catholic specialty, one might learn something new about it. But they are very naturally conservative about the teaching of religion—after all, the Church has been teaching religion for hundreds of years—and there are few who realize that the way it is now taught was unknown until quite recent times.[9] Consequently, many of those in positions of authority are reluctant to release special personnel to study and implement the work of modern catechetics; they simply do not see the need.

"If, during the current academic year, there are enrolled in U. S., Canadian, and European faculties for the M.A. degree or its equivalent fifty full-time U. S. students, and for the Ph.D. and S.T.D. degrees . . . twenty-five students, the primary purpose of whose training is catechetical, the estimate will have been set high; yet in no other field of preparation . . . is the record of Catholic educators so undistinguished." [10]

Only a few institutions in the country offer regular courses in religious education. In spite of valiant

[9] See Sloyan, *op. cit.*, p. 95.
[10] Gerard S. Sloyan, "Catechetical Renewal," *Worship*, XXXVII, January 2, 1963, p. 98.

efforts by individuals and by the Sister Formation Movement—whose aim is to have all religious receive a balanced and continued spiritual, intellectual, and professional training—it is still too generally supposed that any priest or religious is automatically equipped to teach religion on the elementary or high school level. In registering for a course in religious education inaugurated for the summer of 1963 at Mount St. Mary College in Hooksett, New Hampshire, one Sister wrote, "I have been teaching religion for twenty-five years, and this is the first time I will have had any training in how to do it." Since its establishment in 1953, the Society of Catholic College Teachers of Sacred Doctrine has, however, done astonishing work in improving the quality of teaching, as well as in carrying on a searching discussion of the objectives, content, and ordering of college courses.[11]

The situation is due not only to conservatism but also to preoccupation with other educational problems. School superintendents are concerned with problems of building and maintenance, with meeting state requirements and parents' demands as to equipment, curricula, and teacher qualifications. Teachers are obliged to spend their summers in amassing credits toward degrees in education or in a particular subject. Consequently, though more and more people in Catholic education are beginning to be aware that the teaching of religion in Catholic schools has somehow been sidetracked, they seem

[11] See the eight sets of Proceedings of the S.C.C.T.S.D., and its newsletter *Magister*; also Bernard Cooke, S.J., "The Problem of Sacred Doctrine in the College," *Modern Catechetics*, pp. 267ff.

able to do little more than bemoan the fact that there is not enough time to attend to it.

Under these conditions, it is no wonder that the question of how to integrate the whole of education with religious formation has likewise been side-tracked. The pioneer work of Dr. T. E. Shields at the beginning of the century and, more recently, the work of the commission on American Citizenship toward an integrated curriculum for the eight grades of elementary school [12]—have not generally been adopted or followed up. What "integration" exists on this level is mainly along the lines of stressing the Catholic pioneers in American history, including "Catholic words" in spelling lists, introducing priests and Sisters into the stories selected for readers, and asking arithmetic questions about how many Hail Marys would have been said by a class of thirty-five by the time they had recited three decades of the Rosary.

On the high school level, again, in the early 1950's the Christian Foundation at the Catholic University of America developed a series of outlines laying out a unified curriculum. But these outlines have not been incorporated into texts or widely experimented with. On the college level, there has been much discussion [13] and some experiment, but nothing like the attention the question must be given if our

[12] See Sister Mary Nona, O.P., and Sister Joan, O.P., *Guided Growth in Christian Living* (Washington, D. C.: The Catholic University of America Press, 1946).

[13] See, for example, the *Proceedings* of the Catholic College Workshops, 1947-51 (Washington: The Catholic University of America Press).

colleges are to provide the unified Christian formation envisioned by Pius XI.

In brief, here is the situation: While more than a fifth of the priests in the United States, and many more than half the religious, are devoting themselves to the work of providing a general education, along with religious instruction and a religious atmosphere, for a part of the Catholic school- and college-age population, and while vast amounts of pastoral energy, lay effort, and money are being spent for the same purpose, not only the specifically religious instruction of all those not in Catholic schools and colleges, but also the integrally religious *formation* of the young people in Catholic educational institutions, is being neglected.

From the point of view of many American Catholics, the only possible remedy for this situation is to work to improve Catholic education, wherever it needs improving, and to try to extend that same education to all Catholic students. But *is* the Catholic school the only possible solution of the problem of religious formation? History bears witness that the Church has used other methods in the past; might it not possibly use another method in our country today?

2

HINTS
FROM
HISTORY

It is a surprising fact, from the standpoint of the American Catholic experience, that the Church for many centuries managed without anything like a school system. It may be useful, then, to see how it did so, to inquire why Christian schools came into existence in the first place, and to note the particular circumstances that called for the establishment of a Catholic school system in our own country.

During the ages of persecution, the Church obviously was in no position to start schools of its own. But it might naturally be supposed that one of the first enterprises to be undertaken by Christians after the peace of Constantine would have been to establish institutions of some kind for the Christian education of the young. Actually, nobody seems to have thought of anything of the sort. Christian children went right on receiving the available pagan education of the time. By the time of the Emperor Vespasian, this amounted to something like a public school system, at least to the extent that education on all levels was encouraged by the government. Some very elementary training in reading, writing, and arithmetic was provided for almost everyone, and there was a good deal more for those who were better off; grammar, that is, the art of expressing oneself clearly and of reading the classics appreciatively, was taught in the equivalent of our secondary schools, followed by rhetoric and other "higher studies." [1]

This education was centered upon the pagan classics—its core was a word-by-word analysis of Greek and Latin works. But although Christians were well aware of the dangers to Christian faith and morals inherent in an education thus saturated with pagan mythology—Tertullian, for instance, went so far as to say that children were being fed poison and should be taught to reject the poison, and retain only what was good—the idea of establishing Christian schools instead scarcely occurred to anyone.

The reign of Julian the Apostate did produce a temporary exception. When his persecution of Christians called for adherence to the pagan content and spirit of the classics to such an extent that Christians could no longer in conscience attend the schools, some Christian schools were established. An attempt was made to substitute the Christian for the pagan classics: the Pentateuch was rewritten in the style of Homer, the New Testament as a series of Platonic dialogues, and so on, with the intention of giving the same kind of literary training as was provided by the classics. But Julian's persecution was short-lived; once it was over, nobody seems to have thought the experiment worth continuing.

The only known attempt to set up a specifically

[1] See H. I. Marrou, *A History of Education in Antiquity* (New York: Sheed & Ward, 1956).

Christian church school occurred about the year 372, when the Emperor Valens exiled two priests from Edessa to Antinoe in the wilds of the Thebaid. Here one of them started an elementary school as a kind of missionary project, selecting passages for dictation and recitation from the Psalms and the New Testament, and also teaching some sort of catechism.

Yet, centers of Christian "higher studies" were not uncommon. Some came into being as early as the middle of the second century, but soon faded away. St. Justin, the first professed Christian "philosopher," established a regular "school" like those of the pagan philosophers, where he was listened to by Christians and pagans alike. Clement of Alexandria and Hippolytus of Rome, among others, taught in the same fashion, giving what we today would call "lectures" for a general audience—a kind of adult education, in fact.

Origen, in the third century, for a time gave an advanced "class" in the exegesis of Scripture and theology, in addition to the elementary instruction of those preparing for baptism which he conducted as the official catechist, under the auspices of the bishop. But this "class" lasted for only about fifteen years, and during its existence was the cause of great controversy. Generally speaking, whoever wanted special training in what we today would call "sacred studies" received it through personal contact with some learned and holy man. Each bishop, moreover, gathered about him a group of clerics, in which future priests were trained; St. Augustine took a further step toward the organization of what we would call a "seminary" by setting up for all the clerics attached to his cathedral a kind of monastery where the future priests and bishops under his supervision were trained in the study of sacred Scripture and in their pastoral duties.

There were, then, no Christian schools in our sense of the term during those first centuries. And— what is even more surprising—apparently there were no special classes, or any other provision for the Christian formation of the young. The nearest thing to a Christian educational institution, in our sense of the term, was the catechumenate in which pagans were instructed. For this group, a catechetical school —that is, instruction preparatory to baptism, given by an authorized teacher—such as Origen conducted at Alexandria, seems to have become part of the regular setup of every church.

But the instruction given in a catechetical school did not consist of a series of lessons designed to give an intellectual grasp of the truths of the faith. Rather, it was the proclamation of God's great deeds throughout sacred history and an opening out of the Christian way of life. With this process were combined a series of rites—those now telescoped into one ceremony in the present baptismal rite for children and recently redivided into stages in the baptism of adults —in which the Church acted on and prayed for the candidate to obtain for him the graces needed to transform his life and prepare him to receive the enlightenment of Christ.

A catechumen, or "learner," was enrolled after his sincere desire to become a Christian had been vouched for by a member of the Christian community. He might spend months or years in the preliminary stage of the catechumenate. Finally, when he felt ready, and was considered so by the authorities, to take the decisive step of a complete break with his pagan past, he was enrolled for the intensive course of preparation for baptism. This took place each Lent, and was tied in with the Lenten observance of the whole Christian community, proceeding step by step toward baptism on the holy night of Easter.

However strange it may seem to our present ways of thinking, until they actually received the sacraments the only instruction given these candidates concerning those sacraments was that provided by their long familiarization with Holy Scripture. It was during their reception of baptism, confirmation, and the Eucharist, at what we today call the "Easter Vigil," and during Easter week in connection with the daily celebration of the Eucharist, that the bishop's homilies unfolded to them—mainly in terms of the key events of salvation history—the meaning of the sacred signs they were now experiencing for the first time in their lives.

What is perhaps still harder to understand today is that the Christian formation of the newly baptized was considered only to have begun with their Easter-night initiation into the full Christian life. The Christian life itself, centered in the Eucharistic celebration, was meant continually to form each Christian and the whole Christian community so that they would "grow up in all things in Christ." To read the present Propers of the Sunday Masses—the elements of which were largely formulated in those early centuries—from this point of view is to be struck by the many references to progress, growth, and dynamism in the Christian life. Individual Christians, and the whole community, are continually to prepare themselves by prayer and by good works for the glorious return of the Lord. We see it pointed out again and again that each Christian can and should continually become more fully aware of the implications of his baptism, that he can and should continually grow in the "knowledge of Christ": the personal knowing of Christ living and active in His Church, and in the penetration of His "Mystery": Christ as the center of sacred history and of the history of each person: "Christ in you, your hope of glory."

The celebration of the sacraments could be such a formative influence, first of all, because the sacramental rites clearly signified to the people what they were effecting: baptisms were performed in an actual pool of warm, perfumed, flowing water, similar to those in the public baths of the period. Each year the faithful could experience, at the Easter Vigil, the wonder of the sacramental bath undergone by new candidates; they could understand the effects of this bath in terms of the sacred history with which they were familiar. In the same way, the materials for the Eucharist were the bread they ate daily and the wine that was their drink at home, prepared and brought by the faithful themselves to be transformed into the food and drink of immortality.

In addition, for each of the rites, and in connection with the Scripture passages read before the Eucharistic sacrifice, the bishop or one of his assistants gave a sermon which opened up to the faithful the "Mystery of Christ" that had already been proclaimed and communicated to them in the inspired words of Scripture and in the rites themselves. We have only to read some of the homilies delivered to ordinary congregations—those, for example, of St. Augustine, St. Leo, or St. Gregory the Great, with their simplicity of style and depth of thought—to appreciate the quality of Christian understanding which these great pastors presupposed in their hearers. And those hearers were, it seems, eager ones. St. Augustine frequently apologizes for having kept his audience so long—usually over an hour, and there were no seats!—but says that his hearers' interest would not let him stop.[2]

It is sometimes said that the faithful of ages other than our own were interested in religion because they had nothing else to be interested in. Anyone who believes this to be true of the first Christian centuries is obviously unfamiliar with the life of the Roman Empire. There were circuses, games, plays, and pageants; the complex life of a highly developed civilization in its decadence had about as many amusements and distractions, in fact, as we have today. The difference is not that there was a vacuum which religion filled, but rather that the Christian religion was interesting in itself—continually interesting, because the Christian life was thought of as something profoundly and dynamically transforming.

In any event, we can now see how the Christian children of those centuries were formed to the Chris-

[2] See S. Van der Meer, *Augustine the Bishop* (New York: Sheed & Ward, 1961), pp. 391, 427ff. St. Augustine's excitable African audience would now and then interrupt him with cheers when they particularly liked what he was saying—a thing few modern givers or hearers of sermons have experienced!

tian life without any schools or special classes. Their parents gave them their elementary instruction in sacred history and the Christian life; beyond this, they were formed by taking part in the community worship and in the active charity and concern for the whole Christian and human community which centered in and flowed from that worship. In those days, as in ours, there were of course not only fervent Christians but others less fervent, including the lukewarm and the apostates. But it can hardly be said that the quality of the Christianity of those times was inferior to our own.

It was the requirements of worship and prayer on the one hand and of the priestly ministry on the other that first brought Christian schools into being. The reading and meditation of Holy Scripture and the praying of the Divine Office, along with the communal celebration of the Eucharist, constituted the very substance of Western monasticism. It followed that every monk or nun had to be able to read. But as the darkness of barbarianism descended over the dying Empire, fewer and fewer candidates for the monastic life knew how to read before they entered. A school was therefore needed in every monastery to teach them what was necessary for a life of Christian prayer, and also to teach the young children brought to the monastery to be reared there and to become monks later if they wished.

But the concept of "reading" in the ancient world did not mean scanning a text with one's eyes and being able to answer questions about its factual content. It meant seeing the relation of each word to every other, both as to grammar and as to literary effect. And the Christian reading of Scripture meant the same thing in the deepest as well as the broadest sense: it meant penetrating the meaning of the sacred text in reference to the whole plan of salvation and in reference to all human life, including one's own. So, as time went on, the old classical learning came to be revived to some extent in the monastic schools; the monks learned not simply to read but to read analytically and appreciatively, and to express themselves clearly and effectively in order to share their spiritual insights with one another. Monastic education, in other words, was designed to provide the Word of God with alert hearers, who would receive it with cultivated minds and hearts, in order to bring forth the best fruit possible.[3]

Meanwhile, the needs of the priestly ministry were giving increasingly definite shape to that other early institution for Christian teaching, the episcopal school. Bishops had always surrounded themselves with a body of clerics, and it was in such a body that boys and young men were formed for the priestly life—along quite definite lines by St. Augustine, for example. As the Empire and its culture gradually collapsed, educated candidates became rarer and rarer; the bishop had to supply even elementary education in order to ensure that there would be priests with the ability to read the liturgical books and Scripture.

In the sixth century this kind of education was, in theory at least, extended to all parishes. The Second

[3] See Jean Leclercq, *The Love of Learning and the Desire for God* (New York: New American Library, 1962).

Council of Vaison in 529 commanded "all parish priests to gather some boys around them as lectors, so that they may give them a Christian upbringing, teach them the Psalms and lessons of Scripture and the whole law of the Lord and prepare worthy successors for themselves." [4] As Marrou says, this might be called the origin of the modern public school, since many boys attended these parish schools who did not actually become priests, and some went on to one or another learned profession. For although during the Middle Ages the clergy were considered the educated class, learning was even then by no means confined to them; rather, from the monastic, episcopal, and parish schools it spread out to leaven medieval life as a whole. As has often been pointed out, the Church was the first to conceive the ideal of democratic education, in the sense that anyone, from any social class, with or without financial resources, could become learned if he had the desire and the capacity to do so.

It was in certain episcopal schools, made famous by one or more great teachers, that the medieval universities had their origin. Like the episcopal schools themselves, these universities were soon providing professional training not only for priests but for lawyers, doctors, and lay teachers as well.

During these centuries from the collapse of the Empire down through medieval times, the focus of Christian formation for all the faithful gradually shifted. The liturgy remained in Latin, but Latin was no longer the language of common speech. For this and

---

[4] Quoted in Marrou, *op. cit.*

29

other reasons, which will be considered in the following chapter, the sacramental signs became unintel-
ligible, or "mysterious" in our present sense of the
word—sacred actions which the faithful simply looked
at in wondering awe, rather than sacred actions involving them as participants. The liturgy no longer
served to form the faithful immediately and directly,
as by its very nature it was intended to do;[5] receiving
the grace conferred by the sacraments was separated
from understanding the meaning of that grace
through the sacramental signs. Growth in the "knowledge of Christ" came to be considered the privilege of
monks, not of all Christians as such, and to take place
primarily apart from the sacramental celebrations by
means of private prayer and meditation.

But, as the liturgy itself ceased to be a formative
influence, a pattern of social life grew up, organized
around the feasts and seasons of the Church which
became, and, until modern times, remained the chief
means of forming Christians generally, whether they
were educated or not. Formal education, then, although certainly of concern to the Church, took its
place in the general pattern, the "medieval synthesis"
of thought and social life. We are tempted to look

[5] Since so many people still equate "liturgy" with its externals,
and dictionaries tend to confirm this idea, it may be enlightening
to quote the definition given in the Constitution on the Liturgy
approved by the Fathers at the first session of the Second Vatican
Council. "It is the exercise of the priesthood of Christ, in which,
by means of sensible signs, there is signified and, in a way proper
to each liturgical action, there is effected the sanctification of
men, and at the same time the Mystical Body of Christ, Head and
members, performs the full public worship of God." (C. Vagaggini,
L'Osservatore Romano, December 8, 1962.)

back nostalgically on that synthesis as the ideal Christian state of affairs. Yet it had its great deficiencies. Such a total molding of life by religio-social forces tended to minimize the necessity for each Christian's *personal* response to Christ, to place emphasis rather on belonging to the visible Church and receiving its benefits, in this way making religion a matter of conformity and habit rather than of inner conviction. Nevertheless, it seemed like such a complete solution that the myth of "the thirteenth, greatest of centuries" still haunts Catholic thinking.

When the pioneer Spanish friars first came to the New World, they tried to establish a similar Christian pattern of life among the unlettered Indians, and for a time succeeded admirably—notably in the California missions. The Jesuits also, in Canada and parts of the United States, tried to set up Christian villages where the pattern of life as well as instruction in the faith would help to form the Indians as Christians.

But elsewhere, especially along the Eastern seaboard, things were of course very different as nascent American civilization developed. Here various Protestant denominations were trying to establish each its own way of life, and in general these denominations mistrusted Catholics even more than they mistrusted one another. The idea of a pluralistic society emerged only gradually. (In fact, a history of early times might be written in terms of the conflict between the ideal of one or another specifically religious way of life and that of American freedom as we conceive it today.) The situation of Catholics was, then, in some ways comparable to the situation of the early Christians confronting an alien civilization—except that this time it was a civilization in the making, not one in its decline, and it was not a pagan civilization but a composite of warring views of the Christian life and of human life itself.

At the same time, the situation was comparable to that of early medievalism in that no education was provided by the state. Under such conditions the establishment of seminaries was, of course, a basic need everywhere. Our first colleges, Protestant and Catholic alike, were similar to the early medieval parish and episcopal schools in that they originated to train candidates for the ministry or the priesthood—as the *Christo et Ecclesiae* on the original Harvard seal testifies. And general education, at first closely connected with religious formation, was equally a work undertaken by all religious denominations.

The need for education was in most places so clear and so great that in the early days there seems to have been little friction between Catholic schools and those of other denominations. People were only too happy to have any kind of school established that would provide young people with the elements of learning.

Yet anti-Catholic prejudice was generally strong, and it was enormously increased during the nineteenth century by the arrival of Catholic immigrants in vast numbers. Given the predominantly Protestant character of American society at that time, therefore, when cities or states began to establish compulsory education for all children, this seemed to Catholics to include an attempt to educate the children of Catholic immigrants away from Catholicism and toward some form of Protestantism.

The first moves in the direction of secular public education, made in Massachusetts toward the middle of the last century, stemmed from Horace Mann's desire to eliminate from the schools the contradictions between different Protestant tenets, and to substitute a kind of ethical culture with biblical overtones. At about the same period a bitter controversy over Catholic schools arose in New York City, where Bishop Hughes had sought and very nearly obtained public support for Catholic schools—something by no means unheard-of elsewhere at that time, for example, in Poughkeepsie, New York. When that support was finally refused he began a campaign to make the public schools less Protestant so that the beliefs of Catholics attending them would be in less danger; and Catholics have been involved in similar campaigns ever since. (We can therefore sympathize quite easily with the efforts of some Jewish groups today to prevent their children from being subjected to specifically Christian influences in the public schools.)

But at the same time Bishop Hughes began also to devote his energy and that of the Church to the establishment, as rapidly as possible, of Catholic elementary schools. His feeling on the need for such schools was so strong that to every priest whom he appointed as a pastor he would say, "You must proceed upon the principle that, in this age and this country, the school is before the church." [6]

Thus the great push for the establishment not

[6] Quoted by Rev. J. A. Burns in *The Catholic School System in the United States* (New York: Benziger Brothers, 1908).

simply of Catholic schools but of a Catholic school system, as an intrinsic part of the organization of parishes and dioceses, had its beginning. The Third Plenary Council of Baltimore in 1884 fully endorsed Bishop Hughes' policy by decreeing that every pastor was to establish a school within two years unless given special permission for a delay; and Catholic parents were required to send their children to these schools wherever they were available, though it was also made clear that the prescription was not binding under pain of sin.

To help carry out this directive there were various attempts at a solution which would provide state support. One of these was the "Poughkeepsie plan," under which the local board of education leased the parochial school buildings from the parish, maintained the buildings, paid the teachers, and had the right of inspection and control. This plan was in operation for some time, but was finally blocked by a school superintendent who objected to the religious habit worn by the teaching Sisters.

Another solution, the "Faribault plan," was worked out in the diocese of St. Paul under the leadership of Archbishop Ireland, between the pastors and school boards of Stillwater and Faribault. The arrangement was almost the same as at Poughkeepsie, except that religious instruction was given only after regular school hours. This plan became the center of a controversy involving the right of the state to control education as opposed to the rights of the Church and of individual parents, some authorities holding that the Faribault plan unduly compromised the rights of the Church. The effect was to make Catholics suspicious of the Faribault plan and to prevent them from generally advocating its adoption, although an arrangement not unlike it is still in force in some places where Catholics constitute the overwhelming majority of the population.

Certainly, the Church has never been happy with the financial burden of parochial schools; scattered attempts have repeatedly been made to gain whole or partial state support. But in the debate now in progress the lines of argument have shifted. A good deal of the current reasoning is based on the rights of private schools to exist, and on the need to stop the monolith of public education from occupying the entire field. Previously it has more often been argued that the parochial school system is in effect a Catholic public school system, educating children who would otherwise go to the public schools; in fact, as recently as 1954 Theodore Maynard could write in his *Story of American Catholicism* that Catholics "will never cease to protest that they desire to have their schools incorporated into the public school system, or that they will cooperate with the system as soon as the principle of secularization has been removed." And although there are some who object to Catholic schools as being in the same category as private schools and therefore "divisive," through the years the main opposition to the parochial school system has been from those who see it as a rival to that of the public schools—one that not only takes children away from a common educational center but also withdraws a considerable number of citizens from taking any interest in the problems of the public schools.

Again, the argument for state-supported religious schools today is based on the fact that the public schools have become "secular." If, however, we are to look intelligently at our present Catholic school system, we need to realize how different the situation was during the last century, at the time it originated. Then the public schools were by no means either "secular" or neutrally Christian. The public schools inculcated Protestant tenets and, in addition, were often militantly anti-Catholic in their presentation of history and in the literature children were given to read. (Anyone who, even forty years ago, studied English history first in a Protestant private school and then in a Catholic one knows what this can mean: Good Queen Bess could hardly be recognized as the same person from one course to the other.)

A particular cause of controversy at that time was the reading of the King James version of the Bible in the public schools. In our own day Catholic and Protestant scholars are agreed on the literal meaning of Scripture to such an extent that a common version is already in preparation. Many Catholics feel today that any Bible reading in schools would be better than none. But the situation was quite different during the last century. Since the Church had not authorized the King James version, for Catholics its reading could only mean an endorsement of the principle of private interpretation of the Bible.

More important still, the immigrants whose children attended the public schools were in no position to correct or supplement what their children were taught. Many of them had never even seen a Protestant before coming to the New World, and had been hardly aware that there were Christians other than Catholics. The Irish were the only large body of Catholics who spoke the language of the country. Bishop Hughes consequently had reason for his strong conviction of the importance of Catholic schools. But it should be noted that although Bishop Hughes' policy was finally adopted at the Third Council of Baltimore, not all Catholic leaders of the time saw things precisely as he did. Archbishop Williams of Boston, for one, never pushed for the establishment of Catholic schools, and Archbishop Ireland remained convinced of the possibility of co-operating with the public school system.

From our present point of view we can see that the Catholic school served several purposes. Not only did it protect Catholic children from anti-Catholic teachings which their parents, many of them immigrants, were in no position to correct or controvert; but it also helped to solve the problem, perhaps not so consciously perceived, of keeping the children of those immigrant parents from being flung all at once into the main stream of American life and mores. The different racial groups had very different goals; whereas some wished to preserve their religio-cultural identity, others—the Irish above all—sought to retain their religion and at the same time to become Americanized as quickly as possible. But it may be said in general, though far more of some groups than of others, that the parochial school at that period served to slow up the process of acculturation, to make it less of a traumatic experience—less of a complete, almost instantaneous break with the European past and all it stood for. The children in the Catholic schools were "Americanized"—but by teachers of their own race and religion, who clung in great part to old ways, only slowly adopting the new.

At the same time the "national" parishes[7] themselves tried, with varying degrees of success and for varying lengths of time, to set up something like the religious pattern of life which had obtained in Germany or Poland or Italy, with the services and feasts of the Church at the center of social life. As time went on, of course, more and more broke away from this pattern, and the confusion of racial patterns with religion unfortunately meant for many that in breaking away from the old ways they broke away from the Church as well. On the other hand, in the attempt to keep the faithful safe, to protect them from harmful influences, parish life itself has become more and more social and less and less religious. It is not the feasts of the Church—other than Christmas—which provide the focus of attention in parish life today; rather, it is the school or C.Y.O. basketball games, the Knights of Columbus bazaar, the Holy Name raffle.

The parish school itself has been—as will be noted in a later chapter—a powerful factor in this development, for wherever there is a parish school, its interests have almost necessarily become predominant in parish life. But in any event the "national" parish and the "national" school seemed, to those who established them in the last century, a necessity if the faith

---

[7] By a "national" parish is meant one organized for a particular cultural group, sermons and so on being given in the native language rather than English. The typical "American" parish was at one time (and is in some places even today) regarded as "Irish" by these other groups.

and cultural values of Catholic immigrant groups were to be preserved.

This fact may help to explain why today, in an entirely changed situation, it is the comparatively affluent and educated young Catholic homeowners in new suburbs who press their pastor and bishop for Catholic schools. Their obvious motivation is the desire to obtain for their children the Catholic education on which the Church has so strongly insisted since the Third Council of Baltimore. That they are moved by very real faith and zeal to fulfill their parental obligations there can be no doubt. But on a less conscious level, other motivations may also be operative. For these Catholics, their own original racial groupings or those of their parents and grandparents have been irrevocably left behind; they have joined the movers-around and movers-up in our mobile society. It may be, then, that the parochial school is a symbol of both social and religious security, to be clung to in an otherwise chaotic world. These Catholics want their children to have the same kind of emotional security they had, or wish they had had. And to them the symbol of this security may well be the Church as incarnated in the parish school, directed by the pastor and staffed by Sisters. (Lay people are, in the main, still mistrustful of lay teachers; they vastly prefer Sisters or Brothers even if no question of salary is involved.)

We have, then, three situations and solutions from the past to guide our thinking about the problems of Catholic formation in the present. First, there was the situation of the early Church in a pagan society, which provided a pagan education. Here the Church had no schools, not even any "classes in religion" for anyone except catechumens, but it did have an intense religious life, centered in a communal worship which was by its very nature formative of the individual and the community.

Second, there was the situation of the medieval Church, in which society and the pattern of life were themselves Christian, and people were formed both as members of the Church and as members of their society simply by living in that society. Here Christian schools grew up to serve the needs of both the contemplative and the active life, of worship and prayer, and of what we today would call "the apostolate."

And third, there was the situation of the Church in this country during the nineteenth century and the early decades of the twentieth: in the midst of a predominantly Protestant society, hostile both to Catholicism as such and to the traditionally Catholic immigrant groups, the Church established a school system of her own and attempted to establish a parochial life which would keep Catholics away from harmful influences, enabling them to preserve their faith and some semblance of a Catholic pattern of life.

The situation of the Church in our country today is clearly no longer the same. The tone of society is no longer positively Protestant; active hostility to the Church is a thing of the past; Catholics and predominantly Catholic racial groups are now considered as American as anyone else. While Catholics, like Protestants and Jews, may still tend to form separate social groupings, we are all subject to the same mass media and the same cultural influences as other Americans; in our working lives and other spheres of activity we mingle with people of all faiths and of no faith at all. Either with or without a school system of their own, Catholics cannot keep or be kept apart from the general stream of American life.

Nor has the Catholic Church in the United States today very much in common with the situation of the Church during the Middle Ages. Catholic authorities are increasingly aware that Catholics have no right to try to hold general society to the Church's norms of morality by means of state laws. Far less could Catholics make an externally Catholic pattern of life the pattern for society today. Sunday remains society's official day of rest, even though religiously it is so for Christians and not for Jews; Christmas is a secular as well as a Christian feast. But in our society little else remains of the various observances that once molded and pervaded daily life with a religious orientation; moreover, if we take our pluralistic society seriously, we cannot seriously desire the establishment of anything like either the medieval or the nineteenth-century Protestant pattern.

During recent decades, scattered couples and experimental groups have made attempts to set up an integrally Catholic life modeled, very broadly speaking, on the medieval pattern. The Catholic Worker movement, for example, has inspired some families to move to rural areas and there to try to bring about an interweaving of daily life with Christian customs. For several years the magazine *Integrity* exerted an influence in a similar direction, as did the Grail in its earlier stages. All these experiments, however, led to the same discovery of the essential elements of the Christian life—participation in the sacramental life of the Church, prayer, and the exercise of Christian love of neighbor through one's work in the modern world, rather than apart from it—as distinct from any external pattern. With the urging by Pope Pius XII and Pope John XXIII that Catholics take a full and active part in all the manifestations of modern life, it has become clear that to set up a separate culture of our own is not what Catholics are called to do today. The problem of Catholic formation, then, cannot be solved, as it was in the Middle Ages, by the all-pervading influence of religious and social custom.

But the situation of all the Christian churches today does have much in common with that of the early Church. The similarities between our present civilization and that of the late Roman Empire have been pointed out in many other connections. Our society is not officially pagan: the respectable American is not asked to pay divine honors to pagan gods or emperors; it is expected rather, that he will belong to one of the three "major" faiths, Protestant, Catholic, or Jewish, or be an agnostic. But the tone of society in fact is neither pagan nor Protestant nor Jewish, for its attention is centered on man, not on God and man's relations with Him. We might call it anthropocentric, or use the current term "secular humanism" without any connotation of deliberate opposition to religion. In any event, the state now provides an education much more complete and universal than was available in Roman times. And just as the pagan humanism of Greco-Roman civilization provided its special "preparations for the Gospel," so today's secular humanism may well be offering its own. As the Christians of the early centuries could profit from the pagan education of their time, making their own contribution to human learning, communicating with their pagan neighbor—by means of a common vocabulary and common patterns of thought—and thus sharing the light of Christ with them, perhaps Christians could act in the same way today in regard to the secular education and learning of our own age.

If so, the time has come to examine afresh the way in which the early Church formed Christians both old and young, with a view to its possible application. Already there has been a convergence of many lines of thought—theological, scriptural, catechetical, pastoral—toward a belief that participation in the sacramental rites of the Church is, by the very nature of Catholic faith, the focus both of Catholic life and of formation in that life.

With the example of the early Church in mind,[8]

[8] And not only the early Church. In our own times, in the diocese of Meissen behind the Iron Curtain, a pastoral program—even under pre-Council conditions—to make the Mass and the Word of God the sources of Christian life and strength which it is their nature to be has succeeded in keeping the Faith alive and vital under incredibly difficult conditions, with practically no other aids. See "The Liturgy and the Word of God on Parish Life in the German Diaspora," *The Liturgy and the Word of God* (Collegeville, Minnesota: The Liturgical Press, 1958). The same potential of the liturgy seems to be actualized within Russia itself; see Harold J. Berman, "The Russian Orthodox Church," *Harvard Alumni Bulletin*, November 24, 1962.

we cannot dismiss as a wild fancy the idea that participation in the worship of the Church—understood in a far fuller sense than has been possible in recent centuries—could once more become the central and most important formative force affecting all members of the Christian community, and that around this focus other means of religious formation could be organized to supplement and extend it—without the need for also providing Catholic young people with a general education.

Yet confronted with what seems like a totally new idea—especially in the field of religious life and practice—everyone is afraid. We naturally tend, here above all, to "always keep ahold of Nurse for fear of finding something worse." Before exploring the possibilities of some adaptation of the early Christian solution, we need to see what we are afraid of losing if we give up our present pattern in order to try another. We need to see in greater detail why and how the Church in our country has become so wedded to its school system that even to propose that we might get along without it seems perilously near to questioning an article of faith.

The next chapter, therefore, will be concerned with examining the mentality in which the school system grew up, and the influence which it has consequently exercised on its students, on the Catholic community, and on the community as a whole. In this light, we can better estimate how much of our reaction to the idea of a Christian formation given apart from schools is actually "superstition," in the etymological sense of a holdover from a point of view which has lost its former relevance. It may then be possible to

44

appreciate more clearly both the new situation of the Church today and the new point of view—the new synthesis of religion and life now coming into being —and to see not only what these demand in the way of Christian formation but also how their demands may be met.

3

IT
ALL
GOES
TOGETHER

*The Mentality Behind the Catholic
School System*

To MANY Catholics, it seems unthinkable that any
other approach to the problem of Christian formation
might work better than the Catholic school system,
precisely because within its own frame of reference
that system has been so successful. Since the immigrant groups first came to this country, the faith has
not been lost. The Church has flourished. We have
a generous laity, crowded churches, and more men
regularly attending services than in almost any other
country; seminaries and novitiates are filled with
candidates. The typical Catholic is no longer poor,
ignorant, un-American; he is reasonably well off,
reasonably well educated, and as American as anyone else. The Catholic school system has been a
factor in helping to bring all this about and in keeping its members loyally Catholic through all the
changes in their social and economic status. If the
Catholic school system has served the Church so well

46

in the past, why is there any reason to think that a drastic change is needed?

According to this way of thinking, the fact that so many young Catholics seem bored with religion and cynical about the priestly or religious life; or that so many Catholics hold laissez-faire economic ideas condemned by the Church, and right-wing social doctrines completely at odds with papal teaching; or that so many are uninterested in the problems of racial injustice, in society's caring for its sick and aged, in the desperate plight of peoples in other parts of the world; or that there is a continual leakage from the Church, again of unknown proportions— all of this is to be blamed on the influence of modern "secularism." There is nothing to be done against it except to keep working hard and devotedly along the same lines as in the past: providing Mass and the sacraments as conveniently as possible; encourag- in devotions old and new, along with spiritual "refreshers" in the form of retreats and missions; inveighing against immoral modern practices such as birth control and indecent dress; and fostering the Catholic school system as the very heart of the Church's endeavor to keep its children true to the faith in the dangerous maelstrom of modern life.

But even more than the apparent success of our education in the past, what keeps many Catholics from even considering the possibility of Catholic life without a school system is the fact that the mentality in which our school system grew up, and which it tends to perpetuate, makes that system seem to be the obvious solution and thus to rule out any other. This mentality was described many years ago as the

47

attitude inevitable during a "state of siege" [1]—the state in which the Church has felt itself to be from the Reformation up to the present time.

People in such a situation are not primarily concerned with the quality of the life led within the city or with the values being defended. Everyone's attention is on the attacking force and on how the city is to hold out against it. It was in this atmosphere that the still-prevalent forms of religious instruction were first worked out in detail;[2] the clergy above all, but also the faithful, needed to be equipped with weapons of defense against the Protestant teachings which were opposed to Catholic doctrines. And so, on the one hand, very little stress was put on doctrines which Catholics and Protestants hold in common, and on the other, the life Christ gives to His Church was not the object of much attention. The faith had to be defended; the life of the faith had to get on as best it could.

After the violence of the Reformation had died down, a new state of siege was brought about by the Enlightenment. The very existence of God was treated as something to be proved, along with the

[1] The phrase originated with William George Ward, grandfather of Mrs. Maisie Sheed of the firm of Sheed & Ward, which has done so much to show us that the siege is over.

[2] Many of their characteristic features, however—especially their analytical, abstract, unbiblical qualities—were inherited from medieval theological tendencies and are to be attributed not so much to the Counter Reformation siege mentality as to the complex process which had begun much earlier, and which will be described very summarily later in this chapter. See Gerard S. Sloyan, "The Relation of the Catechism to the Work of Religious Formation," in *Modern Catechetics*, pp. 63-101.

possibility and actuality of Revelation, the divinity
of Christ and His founding of a Church. (As a
Catholic college student said upon being asked what
he was studying in religion, "Well, we just proved
Christ and now we're going to prove the Church.")
Since the attack seemed to be launched mainly on the
intellectual plane, the defense was organized on the
same plane—rational proofs for all the truths in dis-
pute were worked out and embodied in religion
courses. With the modern questioning of traditional
morals, a new front was opened up; Christian ideas of
sexual morality in particular had to be defended
against modern licentiousness. Thus the accurate
statement, the justification and "proof" of particular
doctrines on the basis of Scripture, tradition, and reason, came to be the important thing in religious instruction; the synthesis of all doctrines into a single
unified view of Christian truth and the Christian life
dropped out of sight.

In a state of siege, moreover, those who cannot be
adequately equipped to fight the enemy are to be
kept safe inside the walls; every aspect of life needs
to be under the direct control of the authorities. So,
in the Church of the last two centuries, the clergy
came to think of themselves, and to be thought of, as
both protectors of and thinkers for the laity.

Obviously, this siege mentality was still further
fostered by the special condition of the Catholic immigrant groups in the America of the last century
and the first decades of our own. This mentality accounts for the defensiveness which has been so predominant a characteristic of American Catholicism,
both in the way the faith is presented even on ele-

mentary levels and in the attitude of Catholics toward other faiths and those who hold them—an attitude which the ecumenical spirit encouraged by the Second Vatican Council has already begun to change.

This mentality also accounts for the authoritarian, "clericalized" structure of American Catholic life. In the Church's turbulent pioneer days during the last century, the evils resulting from the trustee system— that is, a body of laymen elected by the congregation and constituting the legal owner of church property— when misused by unstable priests and their trustees, made strict control of all church matters by the bishop and his representatives seem doubly necessary. Although there was considerable lay activity to begin with, and although laymen conducted many of the early schools and edited Catholic newspapers and magazines, the clergy came to feel more and more that they must decide all questions and conduct all activities in any way related to the Church, and the laity apparently agreed that it was quite normal for them to do so. So, for example, a layman who intends to set up a bookstore specializing in Catholic books feels that he must have the permission of his bishop to do so; or an educator planning a private experimental school for pupils of all faiths feels that she cannot go ahead without the bishop's sanction.

As a result, clergy and laity have come to think of themselves as two distinct species of Catholics—to such a degree that not many years ago a normally most courteous priest could write that the kind of religious education to be given in college and to the adult laity should not be the same as that given to future priests *because* one could not expect the shepherd to get down on the ground and nibble grass with the sheep! Or, as the educator Willis Nutting once put it,[3] according to the present mentality, the clergy and religious are thought of as the real, fully initiated Catholics; the laity seem to be in the position of perpetual catechumens.

Thus, although the peculiar historical circumstances of the last century no longer prevail, the same siege mentality they fostered now sees the Catholic school system as the only answer to the problem of Catholic formation. Here the children can learn the truths of faith and how to justify and defend them; here they can be kept safe from harmful influences; here they can absorb a sense of loyalty both to the Church and to their country; here they can be formed in the American Catholic tradition.

According to this way of thinking, if we did not have our schools, no Catholic children would really learn their religion; all our children would be exposed to alien ideas almost from the cradle; none of our children would be solidly grounded in piety or the moral virtues. Today, when the home seems to exert less and less force for good in children's lives, when secularism seems to be gaining ground everywhere, how much more necessary it is—so runs the argument—to keep as many children and young people as possible under the influence of priests, Sisters, and Brothers as long as possible; how much more necessary it is than ever before to maintain our Catholic school system. Otherwise, as one priest expressed it, "We might as well let the devil take over right away."

[3] *Parents Are Teachers* (Collegeville, Minn.: The Liturgical Press).

This mentality is all the more entrenched and difficult to change because the necessities of conducting our school system have made the school appear to be the keystone of American Catholic life. The typical parochial school today is the center of parish interest; the majority of parish social events are concerned either with events in the school or with raising money for the school. Affairs such as First Communion are naturally organized around the parochial school children themselves. The altar boys are trained by the Sisters from among the children in their school; so are the members of the choir. The parents of these children, consequently, are bound together by actual projects involving the school, as well as by sharing the complex of interests that center around it. And these parents are, generally speaking, the most energetic and zealous lay people in the parish.

These lay people are bound to one another and to their church not so much by a strictly religious interest as by concern for their children and for the material needs of the school and the parish. It is the pastor who is finally responsible for the school; it is the Brothers or Sisters who conduct it. If there is a P.T.A., it rarely has anything at all to say about what goes on in the school, let alone about educational policy. The school thus tends to perpetuate the idea that the laity can be neither fully competent in nor concerned with religion as such, or with the religious education of their own children. The majority of parents are simply grateful that as the result of their efforts to have a parochial school in their parish their children are receiving the best possible religious training, and that they themselves need feel no further responsibility over matters in which they consider themselves incompetent.

This explains the very real fear experienced by the vast majority of Catholic parents at the idea of undertaking their own children's religious instruction. Even parents who are themselves well instructed— perhaps, indeed, these most of all—suffer from this fear and in the current crisis are consequently asking themselves: If the parochial school does not take care of teaching children religion, who will? If the school does not train the children to receive the sacraments regularly, who will? And they are generally quite convinced that in the parochial school the Sisters or Brothers—and of course the priests—can alone be trusted to teach the children properly. After all, lay teachers are just people like other laymen—religion is not their business.[4]

And, obviously, the very existence of our schools and the efforts we make to maintain them foster the

---

[4] How deeply this idea is ingrained in our thinking may be gathered from the title of a recent book, *Religion as an Occupation*, by the Rev. Joseph Fichter, S.J. Of course, a priest who devotes the major part of his working day to the priestly ministry may be said to have religion as his occupation; so may the contemplative religious who spends the better part of his working day in prayer. But it is hard to see how religion is the "occupation" of a priest or religious whose chief work is, say, teaching chemistry, any more (or less) than it is of the layman doing the same work— and it is with the problems of such priests and religious that the book is chiefly concerned. The author does mention the difficulty of terminology, and suggests "ecclesiastical functionaries" and "the ecclesiastical occupation" as alternatives—but then what term would he use for, say, a full-time church organist or lay teacher of religion?

idea that it is children alone who need religious instruction and training. A large proportion of our priests and religious are devoting their time to the education of the young; the needs of our schools are very prominent in all our planning and in the conduct of diocesan and parochial life. This is one more manifestation of the "child-centered" mentality that has made children and young people the focus of attention, in the American Catholic Church as in American society generally. And so we naturally tend to feel that if we were to let the children go from our schools, we should soon have no Church left. Are not our children the hope of the future?

This child-centeredness further fosters the assumption that the laity are and can be only childishly Christian. Of the children enrolled in Catholic institutions the vast majority are in elementary schools; very many of these will cease attending Catholic schools after the eighth grade. What is and can be expected of the majority of the laity, then, is something like an eighth-grade level of religious knowledge and maturity. And this further enhances the idea that priests and religious are necessarily the only full-time, fully mature, and responsible members of the Church. Consequently, any solution that would call upon the laity to take an active part in the Christian formation of their own children seems chimerical; how could they do so when they are, generally speaking, only children themselves in religious matters, and quite content to be so?

Finally, the very existence of a Catholic school system continues to foster the idea that Catholics need to be segregated, kept apart from those of other faiths.

The parochial school is in the position of being able to dismiss children who do not prove satisfactory in learning or conduct. As a result, a very powerful means of discipline—one used by parents and teachers alike—is the threat of being sent to the outer darkness of the public school. How powerful it can be may be seen from the ironic dilemma encountered by the mother of a child who badly needed a remedial reading course not given in the parochial school, but who burst into tears every time the subject of her going to the public school came up.

Children so conditioned grow up, then, to think of Catholic school children as a special and privileged group. At the same time, public-school teachers can hardly help resenting a Catholic system which refuses to handle difficult Catholic children, and public-school children, familiar with the rejects of the Catholic school system, may tend to think of Catholics as undesirable.

In the same way, the fact that the parents of Catholic school children are drawn together by their common interests tends to cut them off from their fellow citizens' concern with the public school and all the interests that center on it; the fact that the pastor and his assistants are in charge of a parochial school cuts them off, as potentially influential citizens, from any interest in the public school's problems. This in turn is resented by people concerned with the welfare of the public schools, and marks off Catholics as a peculiar and non-co-operative group, especially in localities where a large proportion of Catholic children attend parochial schools.

Consequently the Catholic school system, although

it is not in the least "divisive" in the sense of alienating young Catholics from American ideals or the American way of life, does tend to foster a kind of socioreligious segregation and the idea that such segregation is a desirable thing.

Thus the mentality of the siege, American style, and the effects of conducting a parochial school system combine to make Catholics regard the system itself as essential and to believe that without it the faith would be lost.

But interwoven with the mentality of the siege, there is a whole way of looking at the faith and living the faith which, at an even deeper level, convinces us that the school is the primary and indispensable instrument of Christian formation. To accept the possibility and the desirability of some other solution, consequently, ultimately means rethinking our inherited view of the faith.

Yet, in the climate of the Second Vatican Council, we must all have become aware of the fact that there may be different and yet equally orthodox ways of looking at Christian truth. The Council was called for the express purpose of "renewing" the way of presenting the faith and the living of the Christian life which has been current in the last few hundred years. There is no disloyalty, therefore, in preparing to implement this renewal by a critical analysis of the mentality in which we were brought up. For if the Council has brought anything home to us, it is the fact that we are members of a Church that lives and works within history, a Church that has an internal as well as an external history. It is not a static organization; it is a living organism, changing and growing through the ages of human history.[5]

But the perennial spring of new growth and vitality is always the same: Christ and the Holy Spirit, present and active in the Church from age to age, moving human minds to seek the answers to new questions in the inspired Word of God as understood in the light of the Church's constant and universal tradition. So today we are beginning to see how one-sided were many of the emphases of the past because of the tremendous movement of the modern Church toward what the French call, untranslatably, *ressourcement*—"re-sourcing," immersing oneself in the original springs of the Church's thought and life, without denying or throwing away any of the genuine growth in the past that developed from these same sources.

In the light of today's "re-sourcing," it appears that for many centuries a process had been going on in the Western Church which tended to conceal many of the dynamic, incarnational values of Christianity as people saw it and lived it. This process began, scholars tell us,[6] with the reaction to Arianism, one

[5] "The theologian must never forget that many theological statements which express absolute and eternal truths need be understood and interpreted in the light of the ideological background of the times in which they were developed. Historical circumstances and concrete problems that had to be resolved often caused a presentation of the truth without perfect balance. Emphasis was placed on one aspect of an eternal truth to the detriment of others, and thus the truth itself did not yield the fullness and depth of its meaning." (Cardinal Augustin Bea, "The Ecumenical Responsibility in Teaching Theology," *The Ecumenist*, I, 3, p. 41.)

[6] See J. A. Jungmann, *Pastoral Liturgy* (New York: Herder & Herder, 1962), Part I.

of the oldest heresies in the Church (again a siege reaction). The Arians denied the full divinity of Christ. The Catholics then began to emphasize it in every possible way, with the result that less emphasis was given to His full humanity. This underemphasis brought about the feeling that Christ is, one might say, wholly on God's side of the interchange between God and man which is the essence of the Christian religion. (Ask the ordinary Catholic child who Jesus is and the answer will be "God"—not "the Son of God made man," or "our Lord," but simply "God.") Christ is thought of as having become man to teach us, to save us from sin, to open to us the gates of heaven. But He is not thought of as having become man to be one with us, so as to take us with Himself and in Himself to God.

Thus Christ's redeeming work was no longer thought of as affecting His own human nature first of all. The idea that it was only through His suffering and death that, as man, He entered into His glory—the glory proper to Him as the incarnate Son—was, as it were, played down lest it seem to detract from His full divinity. And so our union with Him, by faith and the sacraments, by the gift of His Spirit, in His great journey to the Father, was gradually lost sight of. Christians came to think of themselves as struggling individually toward Christ with the helps He provides in the Church, rather than as being members of His Body, sharing His life, sharing in His work, going together in and with Him through His Passion and Cross to His risen life with the Father.

This meant that, as time went on, what might be called the human dimensions of God's self-revelation and self-giving to mankind through Christ in the Church were largely lost to view. Christianity came to seem atemporal rather than essentially historical —the free intervention of God in human history and in the personal history of each man, bringing mankind to Himself anew through the successive stages of the history of salvation. Christians no longer thought of themselves as sharing in the history of salvation, as called and enabled in Christ to take part in carrying out the design of God's love in human history. They no longer saw the redemption as affecting whole human persons, body and soul; salvation seemed to be concerned with souls alone.

Thus the social dimensions of Christianity were lost sight of as well. The final introduction of redeemed mankind, body and soul, into the joy of their Lord at the end of time was no longer thought of as the ultimate fulfillment of each individual Christian's life and work and of God's whole plan. The attainment of salvation came to seem an individual affair. Christians no longer thought of themselves as members of Christ or as members of one another. The radiation of Christ's love in the active service of one's neighbor, therefore, no longer stood out as the great means given us in daily life of expressing our love for God and carrying out Christ's work among men. "Charity" came to seem just one virtue among many; the important thing was strict obedience to the commands of God and the Church.[7]

---

[7] A Catholic college graduate, a teacher in a Catholic college, recently asked a colleague, "Say, did you ever hear this: 'Love is the fulfilling of the law.' Do you know where it comes from?" And

This may help to explain why the social encyclicals of the Popes, from Leo XIII to John XXIII, seem to so many Catholics today to be entirely uncalled for, to deal with subjects outside the purview of the faith. These Catholics are quite convinced that God simply asks us to save our own souls, not to be our brothers' keepers; they do not think of Him as concerned with the quality of human lives led on this earth, or with earthly life at all, but only with "souls"—and the keeping of souls is an affair for priests.

No wonder, then, that the essentially "interpersonal" character of the Christian life was also lost sight of. The Father was no longer thought of as revealing and giving *Himself* to us through Christ, gathering us together to share His life as "sons in the Son"; He was merely telling men truths about Himself and about what men had to do in order to be happy forever. Exceptional Christians might feel that they had been drawn into a personal relationship with Christ Himself, but this came less and less to be regarded as the glorious privilege of every Christian by virtue of his baptism. The Holy Spirit came hardly to be thought of at all—still less the idea that He is the supreme Gift of God's love, pouring out that infinitely generous love in our hearts, so that we can love God and men with God's own love.

Thus ordinary Christians no longer felt drawn together by the dynamism of that love; they no longer felt the necessity of proclaiming the Good News of God's love to those who had not yet heard it. And

when he had been told, he went away muttering, "That's marvelous. Makes you want to read St. Paul!"

so, today, it seldom occurs to the majority of Catholics to feel any special joy in assembling together for Sunday Mass; the "apostolic-minded" Catholic is still a rarity, and is in fact thought rather odd by his fellow Catholics.

It is no wonder, then, that the celebration of the liturgy has come to be thought of simply as the carrying out of our duty to worship God and as a "means of grace." Catholics come to Mass to have Christ made present on the altar and to worship Him, rather than to meet with Him and, with and in Him, to worship the Father in the Spirit. The Mass is no longer thought of as the act of Christ involving all His members, individually and as a community, in His action of worship and redemption; or as the revelation of Christ to His members, through the sacred signs, of who He is and what He asks of them in view of the loving communion of all mankind in the life of God. In fact, one first-grade catechism, bearing two Imprimaturs and still in use in some schools, describes the Mass as "the set of prayers the priest recites to hide Jesus in the Host."

Without the focal synthesis of "Christ in us, our hope of glory," each doctrine has come to be thought of separately, not as one aspect of a single whole. The accurate formulation of separate doctrines has come to seem more desirable, because more accurate and intellectually comprehensible, than God's own word in Sacred Scripture. And so God is no longer thought of as communicating with us through the inspired texts; those texts are something belonging to the past, not God's Word here and now to His people—some-

61

thing to be studied for "proofs" of this or that doctrine and to be used as edifying examples, but not as God's Word to us here and now.

In this way of looking at things, consequently, the truths of faith (other than the existence of hell and heaven) became separated from moral action and the daily conduct of life; they became simply a series of "things we must believe in order to be saved." In turn, leading a moral life was simply what one had to do in order not to go to hell, not the new life Christ enables us to lead as "new men," in the spirit of love. The practice of religion came to mean using the "means of grace"—prayer and the sacraments—which God has given us in the Church, rather than our vital encounter with Christ in the sacramental and prayer life of the Church, forming us to His likeness and enabling us to cooperate with Him. Thus the idea of the Christian life as essentially a life of love faded from view; it became a series of duties. Special devotions to Christ under one or another aspect, or to Mary and the saints, grew up in an attempt to fill the void between faith and human living. And the mentality of the siege came along to add its peculiar qualities of defensiveness and rigidity.

Of course, the recognition that this view of the faith is one-sided and fragmentary is now possible precisely because a more complete view is beginning to replace it—a new synthesis, including all the developments in devotion and doctrine which have enriched Western Catholic life throughout the centuries, but based on the original dynamic Apostolic and Patristic pattern. It is in the light of this new

synthesis that we can understand why, to the view of
the faith current in recent centuries, Catholic schools
should have come to appear the indispensable means
of Christian formation—and likewise why the formation they give seems a very partial one compared with
the more dynamic view of Christian truth and life
that is emerging in our time.

According to the former point of view it is important above all that children learn what they
must believe and do in order to be saved, that they
acquire an urgent sense of "oughtness" about be-
lieving and doing rightly and about using the means
of grace and that, if possible, they acquire some
emotional attachment to religious practices. Where
can this be carried out better than in a school where
the children have religion class five times a week, be
taught by priests and religious, be surrounded with
religious pictures and statues, be made to recite their
prayers and go to confession and Communion regularly, and—at least during school hours—be kept safe
from teachers and students of other faiths?

According to this view the truths of faith are not
meant to be intrinsically interesting anyway; it does
not matter whether or not the children's minds and
hearts are touched by them; the important thing for
young people is to be equipped for life with a correct
way of stating what they must believe and do. And so,
many parents and teachers accumulate a fund of
stories about children's misunderstanding of chate-
chism formulas—stories that would be funny if they
did not represent a truly tragic situation.

There was, for example, the father who came home
one day to find his household in an uproar because

his six-year-old son was saying that his seven-year-old daughter had told him God was a "green bean." She said no, what she had really said was "supreme bean"; that was what she had learned in school. After a moment it dawned on the father what she meant was "Supreme Being." But when he tried to find out what this phrase meant to his daughter, she only grew tearful and exclaimed, "Don't bother me with what it *means*. It's what we have to say when Sister asks us who God is." [8]

How many parents with children in a Catholic school have had similar experiences! Genuine explanations of what the formulas of the catechism mean are seldom possible; the children are pressed for time, they have other homework to do. They do not want their parents to explain the meaning of the formulas, but simply to help them learn them by heart. And so the "things-we-must-believe" approach to religion is perpetuated in yet another generation.

Of course the same approach prevails in Sunday school and other religion classes as yet untouched by the catechetical renewal. But it is far easier for a Catholic who has thus "learned his religion" only in weekly classes apart from his regular schooling to realize later on that he still has much to discover about

[8] There was also the new pastor who did not realize that the children in his school had been trained according to *A Catholic Catechism* (a translation of the new German catechism, a first product of the catechetical reform). He asked a First Communion candidate, "Who is God?" Instead of answering according to the Baltimore catechism formula, "God is the Supreme Being, infinitely perfect," the boy said, "God is our Father in heaven who loves us." "You're wrong," said the pastor.

religion (and that it might be interesting to do so) than it is for a Catholic school product to realize the same thing. The latter naturally assumes that he has had the best, and he hasn't liked it. And so he does not merely suspect, but is nearly always deeply convinced, that religion is boring and unconnected with his real interests. "More of the same old stuff" is his almost invariable reaction to whatever he may be given in high-school or college classes in religion.[9]

In the same way, Catholic schools perpetuate the idea of prayer as the dutiful use of a means of grace, rather than as communication with God our Father and with Christ, our Head and Brother. In most schools the great formulas of Christian prayer are recited mechanically, far too often, and under circumstances that militate against the children's acquiring the spirit of true prayer. One not untypical school, for instance, requires the children to recite the Rosary while they file out for recess. Besides these formulas, children learn and are frequently called upon to repeat "Acts" that are mere abstracts of the content of a living prayer. How little they mean to the children may be gathered from one boy's version of the first line of the Act of Contrition: "O my God, I am heartily sorry for having offended Thee" ren-

[9] A certain type of mind may, it is true, become interested in arguments "proving" the existence of God, the divinity of Christ, and so on. But given this general outlook, such arguments lend themselves to a conviction that everyone outside the Church lacks not only faith but also the power or will to reason logically—a conviction that ignores, among other things, that faith is a *gift;* moreover, these arguments seldom foster an interest in Christian truth as the revelation of God's love.

dered as "O my God, I am partly sorry for having a friend like Thee"!

On the other hand, when other prayers are added, they are too often the expression of a flowery and fervid piety equally unsuited to the child's real self. Even with the progress of the scriptural renewal, as yet few schools have thought of making the children familiar with those inspired prayers of Scripture, the Psalms. And so the children come to feel that prayer is not meant to say anything to God that one might really want to tell Him; one is not meant to be one's real self in praying. They are not formed in the spirit or in the wonderful variety of forms of Christian prayer, and they come to believe that any recitation of a prayer formula is prayer and a "means of grace." So long as one says one's memorized prayers regularly, one's duty to God is fulfilled.

The same thing holds true of receiving the sacraments: The children automatically go to confession and receive Communion every First Friday; they go to Mass on Sunday—during the school year. And when a pastor asks that they begin to "participate" in the Mass, too often this simply means learning more formulas and obediently reciting or singing them at the proper places.

To the mentality inherited from recent centuries, this formalism is regrettable but inevitable. The children must learn the prayers that they will need to say during life, and acquire the habit of saying them; what else can be done?

According to this way of thinking, it is also regrettable but inevitable that some aspects of morality do not seem to "take" with young people today.

Teachers realize all too well that cheating, for instance, is as rife in Catholic schools as anywhere else. The senior examination in ethics at one Catholic college is held in the gymnasium, with two priests patrolling the track above and two more walking around among the students. In another, the exams have to be kept in a locked safe and secret even from the office staff because of students' attempts to force their way into the dean's office and to bribe the secretaries. At another, several professors have given up assigning term papers because they know that so many of them will have been bought or plagiarized. On the lower levels, children whose home training has borne forcibly on this aspect of morality assume that they will sometimes get lower marks than their fellows because they don't cheat in school and their parents won't do their homework for them.

Everyone of course, and rightly, blames the home. But it does not occur to this mentality to try to remedy the situation throughout the educational process by giving moral teaching in the manner of St. Paul and St. John—to show lying and stealing as unworthy of members of Christ, as an offense against love; to show cheating as unworthy, not only because it is a form of stealing and of lying, but because it involves a misuse of the powers a student should be developing to serve God and his neighbor in love. Thus the school does nothing to change the get-ahead-at-all-costs attitude which so many young people absorb from their parents and surroundings. When they grow up and enter the world of adult social relations, of work and business, it is almost impossible for them to understand that some forms of competition are unworthy of a Christian, or that following the principles of *Mater et Magistra* and *Pacem in Terris* is in any way their Christian duty.

Again, Catholic schools make a great effort to bring home to their students the desirability of a vocation to the priestly or religious life. But the mentality inherited from the past is not aware of the worth and the requirements of the Christian vocation as such. And so our schools generally give little direction to students who are not going to become priests or religious as to what they are to do with their lives—aside from staying out of mortal sin, keeping in the state of grace, and so getting safely to heaven. The vocational guidance given in most Catholic schools and colleges goes hardly any further than non-Catholic counseling: What are your aptitudes, tastes, and circumstances; in view of them, in what kind of work will you be happiest and most successful? It does not add the specifically Christian question: In precisely which form of this work will you have the greatest opportunity to grow in the knowledge and love of God, render the fullest service to your neighbor, and so help carry out God's plan for mankind?

Similarly, Catholic schools inculcate a great respect for priests and religious. "Sister says . . ." becomes an unanswerable argument for a first-grader by the end of his first week in school; "Father is going to give out report cards today" is a powerful incentive even to an eighth-grader to polish his shoes and find a clean tie. But the respect thus inculcated is not a realistic one; it does not distinguish the office or the "holy habit" from the person, nor the heroism involved in dedicating oneself as a priest or religious from the actual achievement of perfection. Conse-

quently, in the high-school or college years or later
during adult life, more than a few Catholics become
disillusioned and cynical when they find priests or
religious acting like imperfect human beings. Some
go so far as to leave the faith entirely, concluding
that it has been proved worthless by the human
failings of those who ought to be perfect. They have
never been shown that imperfection in the Church
itself and in priests and religious is taken into account in God's plan (and it does not even occur to
them that if achieved perfection were required of
some of the members of the Church, it would be
equally required of all—including themselves).

Of course, many Catholics do grow up into a more
mature and realistic attitude. But a great deal of the
kind of anticlericalism that does exist stems from
such false notions about what priests and religious
ought to be. At the same time, the way in which
the priesthood and the religious life are presented in
Catholic schools is almost universally successful in
fostering the idea that only priests and religious are
full-time Christians, that religion is properly their
business and not that of lay people. And so another
generation grows up feeling that only priests and
religious can "really" teach religion, that they alone
are really responsible for the life and work of the
Church.

Thus the way in which religion is taught, morality
inculcated, and the ways of Christian life presented
in most of our Catholic schools tends to perpetuate
the way of looking at the faith developed in the last
centuries. Since it seemed for so long the only possible way, many of us naturally find it difficult to look

beyond it. It is, perhaps, peculiarly difficult for American Catholics to do so because in some ways the old outlook seems to fit in so well with one current view of the American way of life. It encourages people to be good citizens and to frequent the "church of their choice." It harmonizes with today's search for security, offering Catholics eternal security if they continue to believe and act rightly. It does not ordinarily interfere with the pursuit of status and success. Only in the unfortunate matters of divorce and birth control (and movies which seem opposed to right morals) does this view of the faith, so far as the layman is concerned, come into conflict with the notions that one's own life is one's own business—that each man *is* an island, that liberty means the right to treat other people in any way one can get away with, and that the pursuit of happiness means the attainment of comfort. This is possibly one reason why so many Catholics are to be found in extreme rightist movements.

It is no wonder, then, that this general outlook on the faith has such a strong hold over American Catholics, priests and laity alike. And it is no wonder that the school system, which is such a powerful factor in perpetuating it, seems to so many Catholics an integral part of the American Catholic way of life, and that questioning its indispensability seems tantamount to questioning the very foundations of the faith.

On the other hand, we American Catholics are noted for our loyalty to the papacy and to the Church. We have shown ourselves generous in responding to whatever has been asked of us. And this is true not only in relation to supplying the material needs of the Church all over the world; American response, for example, to the urging of the Popes, from St. Pius X onward, for more frequent Communion has been outstanding, even though this originally involved a considerable change from the mentality of the last century in relation to reception of the Eucharist.

Now the Church, through the Council, is indicating a further and greater change in our ways of thinking about and living our faith. However radical this reorientation may appear, it is clearly a duty to examine the reasons why it is called for and to undertake it wholeheartedly. In doing so, it may be that some of our most cherished institutions will no longer seem necessary; since they developed in response to a past situation and in accordance with a mentality belonging to the past, they may now be a positive deterrent to carrying out today's urgent tasks. The possibility must at least be considered that the present situation, and the response the Church is calling us to make to it, will eventually relieve us of older burdens in order that we may the better shoulder new ones.

It is in this light that we must examine afresh the whole question of religious formation. In the present situation, who most needs it and of what basically should it consist; what, in fact, is its chief purpose? As the old mentality conditioned the answers given to these questions in the past, so the new mentality, which has been in the process of formation in the Church for many years and which is now being more widely diffused by the Council, must necessarily condition the answers that will be given in the future.

4

WHO
NEEDS
FORMATION?

THE idea that the educational effort of the Church should be directed primarily toward young children has been with us for some time. It can seem very plausible. Even Catholic parents who are not particularly concerned with religion for themselves usually believe that their children should have religious instruction. They are grateful to have their children under good supervision whenever and wherever it is provided. And so it is not too difficult to get hold of children and teach them in schools or, if not in schools, in classes; all this at least is much easier than getting hold of their elders. Children can be made to memorize formulas and to recite prayers; they can be shepherded to Mass and the sacraments.

St. Pius X unwittingly gave a new impetus to the concentration on small children when he lowered the age for receiving First Communion to seven years. (The ancient practice, still observed in the Eastern Churches, is for babies, as soon as they have been baptized, to begin receiving Communion under the species of wine along with their parents, and the Bread as soon as they are capable of swallowing it.)

The idea that preparing the children properly for First Communion is an end in itself still influences many parents; they are eager to have their children in Catholic schools at least until that milestone has been passed. And it is reassuring, when one sees a white-clad First Communion class "looking so sweet," to recall the dictum that if one can get hold of a child for the first seven years, one can set his outlook for life.[1]

However, nearly everyone can see that children really need to learn more about their faith than they can absorb by the age of seven, so that confirmation —normally received, at least in the eastern United States, between the ages of eleven and thirteen—has become in many parents' minds a kind of terminus for their children's formal religious instruction. This affects many of the parents whose children do not go to Catholic schools; they will frequently see to it that their children attend religion classes until they have been confirmed, but make little or no effort afterwards. For this reason, many authorities are reluctant to lower the age for confirmation or to consider

---

[1] When one considers the denial of the power of both free will and grace implied in this notion, one wonders how it has managed to permeate so much of our thinking about Christian formation. And what of the saying attributed to Napoleon, and so often quoted in First Communion sermons, that the day of his First Communion was the "happiest day of his life"? Whether or not this was true of Napoleon—who, after all, must have been considerably older on that occasion than First Communicants have been since the time of St. Pius X—the frequent repetition of this statement sheds light on current notions as to the possibilities of natural and supernatural growth to be expected of ordinary Catholics.

the possibility, as in the early Church and in the oriental practice, of administering it immediately after baptism. Other authorities, on the contrary, consider that it would be advisable to return to the practice of the early Church—thereby, among other things, removing the possibility of considering confirmation as the terminal point of religious formation.

Where schools were concerned, it was quite natural that the Church in this country should have concentrated on providing them for the elementary level during the nineteenth century and the first decades of the twentieth. Since only an elementary education was universally required, it was only on that level that the problem seemed acute.

But the situation is different now. Since by law every child must now go to school until he is sixteen and since only unskilled jobs—if those—are available to young people without a high-school diploma, the focus is shifting to the high schools. Catholics are beginning to wonder whether children do not need a Catholic education during these years even more than in the elementary grades. There is considerable discussion as to whether, if we cannot provide a Catholic education at every level, it would not be wiser to concentrate on the secondary level; in any case, building high schools has become a major concern in many dioceses. And now that a college degree is becoming as necessary to get a good job as a high-school diploma used to be, the question of providing a Catholic college education for more young people is becoming a matter of increasing concern.

At the same time, the needs of the times have already caused us to look beyond educational institutions and classes for children and young people to the needs of their parents. Of course, the Church has always clearly stated that the religious formation of children is primarily the responsibility of their parents. One line of thinking continues to maintain, and very strongly, that the primary way by which parents should carry out this responsibility is to see to it that there are Catholic schools for the children to go to and that they go to them. But we are forced by the present situation to see that this is not enough. On the one hand, as more and more Catholic schools are adopting a policy of discontinuing the lower grades, it is beginning to be urged that parents undertake the religious education of their small children, and be equipped to do so. And on the other hand, the failure of the school, without intelligent and consistent cooperation from parents, is becoming more and more obvious.

Every good teacher admits, and parents are constantly reminded, that the school is virtually helpless without the home. Teachers in parochial schools sigh daily, "You can always tell what kind of a home a child comes from." They know that they can teach doctrinal and prayer formulas, they can enforce discipline in school, they can make sure that a child carries out his religious duties during the school year. But they realize very clearly that unless the parents are seriously concerned about the child's religious formation, he is as likely as not to drop all his good habits during the summer. There are, it is true, certain unusual children who keep up their good practices without family example or encouragement, sometimes almost in spite of their families; but they are rare exceptions. How many parochial school children, for example, fail to go to confession even once during the summer? How often, then, will they go after they have grown up, when there is no one to make sure that they carry out religious practices at all?

Because with the obvious spread of the secularist outlook the effect of parental attitudes has become so clear in recent years, the numbers of sermons, pamphlets, magazines, and books addressed to parents have all been multiplying. A special bureau of the National Catholic Welfare Conference is devoted to the family and its problems. At the same time, the spread of the Cana and pre-Cana movements to foster a greater understanding of all the aspects of Catholic married life among married and engaged couples, and of the Christian Family Movement with its aim of promoting a clearer view of Christian family life and of facilitating human and Christian living in each community, are indications that many parents are eager to find out how better to carry out their complex duties in today's world.

We are, then, already engaged in a widespread effort to form parents as fully Catholic parents. But parents themselves realize that they are persons even before they are parents, husbands, or wives and that they need formation as Christian persons not less than as Christian married persons or as the parents of Christian children. Some priests say that young married people with small children are the most hopeful group to work with since the real problems of adult life are dawning on them: They feel the need to penetrate more deeply into the Christian meaning of life, and to find that meaning in their own lives.

But so far as bringing up their own children is concerned, thoughtful parents realize that their influence by itself is limited. Everyone agrees that while the children are of pre-school age and in the lower grades, their parents are the chief formative force in their lives. Yet even at this early age the children's playmates (and so *their* parents) have an increasing influence, and parents already hear the argument "But everybody does it," or "Nobody does *that*."

As children reach high-school age, these arguments begin to be heard much more frequently and urgently, combined with "*You* don't understand," or "*You* don't know anything about it." By this time the influence of other personalities becomes important—a teacher, a coach, a relative outside the immediate family.

But most important of all is the influence of teen-age society itself. Everyone knows that at this period, to be one of the "in-group" is of crucial importance. Teen-age society itself at once accepts and rebels against the norms of adult society.[2] It tends to accept the hidden norms—status, security, a good time—not those explicitly proposed: purity, generosity, fair dealing. It tends to rebel against formal and arbitrary norms that are not observed by its elders—against discipline applied only to the young, against pietism and "respectability." But in so doing it only conforms in a different way—to a stereotyped kind of rebellion.

[2] See, for example, James Coleman, *The Adolescent Society* (Glencoe, Ill.: The Free Press, 1961).

Now it is not too difficult for an intelligent and zealous parent living in a mainly non-Catholic society, with his children attending non-Catholic schools, to make the point that Catholics have other norms to live by, that they cannot follow their teen-age group in everything, any more than the parents are following their adult neighbors in everything, that they must learn how to accept and follow along with what is good in their society and to stand out, if necessary, against what is not.

But to make the same point cannot help being more difficult when the young people are immersed in a mediocre *Catholic* milieu. If, at the age when adolescents are rebelling against their parents and trying to establish their own identity, their parents' norms appear different from those of other Catholics, they cannot but become confused. Whose norms are they to accept, whose are they to rebel against? In such a situation, the parents can do little more than continue to point out the standards they themselves are trying to live by, not on the basis of parental authority but rather on that of common sense and faith, while praying that what emerges from the confusion will be not indifference but a greater degree of maturity and self-commitment to Christianity.

In view of this situation, every thoughtful parent cannot help praying that the Church's effort to form children and to form parents may be extended to the whole adult community. He knows that his teen-age boys and girls need the opportunity to meet and become acquainted with mature Christian personalities. He knows that he and they need the vital support and inspiration of an adult Catholic community

78

which will present Catholic standards not so much in words as in actions and the total orientation of its life. Under today's conditions, young Catholics see little that is inspiring in Catholic life as it is led by grown-ups in the ordinary parish. How can a boy be really eager for the day when he is mature enough to take part in the meetings of the Holy Name Society or the Knights of Columbus? How can a girl be influenced for good by a desire to qualify for the Altar and Rosary Society or the Ladies' Guild?

Whenever young people today are brought to a vital concern about the Christian life, it is either because of some outstanding personality or through the influence of a movement like the Young Christian Students—a movement of young people, led by elders who are motivated at once by love of Christ and by a genuine interest in young people, and who propose dynamic goals for Christian living and action, goals which they themselves are pursuing. As things stand, a parent can only pray that his children will encounter and respond to such an influence. And this is true whether or not the children attend Catholic schools. Catholic high-school society both imitates and rebels against its elders just as inevitably as does the society of the public high schools.

The renewal of adult Catholic life, the formation of adults, would therefore seem vitally necessary today even if we were thinking only of the ultimate formation of the young. Things may have been different in the past when a certain external pattern of Catholic life still existed; when Catholics generally attended not only Sunday Mass but Sunday Vespers as well; when they flocked to devotions and missions as a matter of course. In those days it may have been possible to lead a good Catholic life without much individual thought or effort; one simply did what all Catholics did. But today, as Pius XI said many years ago, "It is no longer possible for a Christian to be mediocre." If Catholic young people are to become more than mediocre Christians they need the influence and example not only of their parents, but of other Catholics as well; they need a vital religious life into which they can grow and mature; they need to be able to find Christ in others, to see a witness to the reality of His love in other lives, if they are to find it worth while to remain in the Church.

But is this possible? Can adults' ways of thinking and doing things be changed? It should be obvious that they can. All the great religious movements of history have originated among adults and have reached children only through those adults. In any case, God Himself has always acted as though both conversion and growth were possible for grown-ups. The prophets did not address themselves to the children among the "children of Israel." The Law given on Mount Sinai was not given primarily to children, nor was it primarily accepted by them. When St. John the Baptist began to herald the coming of the Kingdom, it was adults whom he called to be "converted." It was adults—soldiers, tax gatherers, ordinary people—who listened to him and were moved by his words to ask what they should do.

When Jesus began to preach the coming of the Kingdom, it was, again, to adults that He addressed Himself. He gathered children around Him certainly; He embraced and blessed them and told His followers that they must be childlike to enter the

Kingdom. But the crowds who followed Him were mainly adults—the children just came along: "There were fed more than four thousand men, besides women and children." His followers were grown men and women; we do not hear anything about children among His close disciples. He must have thought it was possible to form adults, and He must have succeeded in doing so, or there would be no Church.

In the same way, the work of the Apostles was to convert adults and then to continue to form them as Christians. Our New Testament, in fact, was composed for the purpose of forming the whole Christian community, to help all its members grow up in all things in Christ. The few references in the New Testament to the children of the Christian community indicate that they were considered the responsibility of their parents; the "teaching Church" addressed its instruction not to them but to its adult members.

It has been pointed out in a previous chapter that the Church of the first centuries followed the same policy. Great care was taken with the formation of adult converts; the continuing "educational" effort of the Church was concerned with its adult members. More precisely, the educational effort of the Church was one with its inmost life. The faithful were formed in Christ by taking part in the liturgical celebrations; it was in connection with these celebrations that they received instruction from their bishop or priests, an instruction concerned mainly with opening out and applying to their own lives the mystery of Christ revealed and communicated through Holy Scripture and the sacramental rites.

We have, therefore, the witness of both Scripture

and tradition that adults are "formable." Certainly, in many other areas we act as if they were so. Considerable legislation and a vast body of literature exist to promote the continual spiritual growth of the clergy and their advance in the sacred sciences. They must make a yearly retreat; they must attend conferences of the clergy; daily "spiritual reading" is recommended, and so are actual study of Scripture and of the Church Fathers, in addition to a complex program of daily prayer. The clergy, then, are assumed to be capable of continual growth both in their knowledge of revelation and in the spiritual life.

For several centuries, on the other hand, it was assumed that religious who were not priests could grow in the spiritual life without any growth in knowledge. Only recently has more than a minimum catechism knowledge of the truths of faith been given to young religious in the course of their formation. The spiritual reading provided for religious has became solid food rather than pious exhortation. Here the Sister Formation Movement has been making a great contribution; through meetings, conferences, workshops, lectures, publications, and cooperation with related organizations, it is seeing to it that Sisters are given the means to "grow up in all things" in Christ, that spiritual and intellectual growth are both fostered.[3]

For many centuries, also, the adult laity as a whole have been supposed capable of change and growth only on the level of obedience to the commandments

[3] See the *Proceedings of the Sister Formation Conferences,* ed. by Sista Rita Mary, C.H.M. (New York: Fordham University Press, 1956-57-58-60).

—that is, the moral level. They were exhorted to lead better lives and urged to use one or another of the "means of grace" and to provide others with an example of the benefits of so doing. However, they were assumed to have learned as children all they needed or wanted to know about the faith, and growth in the "spiritual life" was considered out of the question for the ordinary layman.

But the last decades have at least begun to disprove these assumptions. It is now generally recognized that adolescents need to be given a more developed knowledge of Catholic truth, and one which will have some bearing on their other studies and their lives. College courses in theology are now a commonplace, although thirty years ago the first attempt by a priest to give some real content to a senior course in religion at a Catholic college for women was looked at as a rather daring as well as unduly optimistic experiment. Discussion is still going on in the various colleges themselves, and in the meetings of the Society of Catholic College Teachers of Sacred Doctrine, as to the purpose, content, and ordering of these courses. Nobody would assert that they are generally successful in awakening in students a desire to pursue the study of Christian truth after they leave college. But at least it is now assumed that college students are capable of acquiring a knowledge of religious truth on a level with their knowledge of general subjects.

In addition, the 1920's and 1930's saw the emergence of "theology for the laity." The concern to make it possible for the laity, now generally "literate" in the broadest meaning of the term, to grow in a knowledge of Catholic truth and its application to life, has become increasingly manifest, even at the pious magazine and pamphlet level, and is producing a multiplicity of good, mediocre, and incredibly poor religious reading material—the poor and mediocre being far more widely read than the good.

This lamentable state of affairs is, of course, not merely a Catholic but a universal American phenomenon. When the Catholics of a small town were about to launch a parish library, the chairman of the venture went to the head of the local public library to explain that their project was not trying to compete with the public library but merely to make books available to Catholics which it was not in a position to buy. The librarian answered almost with tears in her eyes, "We would be only too grateful to anyone who could get the people in this town to read anything besides comic books!"

Her cry is not unique. The anti-intellectuality of the American ethos has been much discussed; it is obvious that our universal education has not as yet succeeded in producing a really literate public. Add to this the impression produced by Catholic teaching—that religious truth is of its nature abstract and lifeless—and it is perhaps remarkable that so many really good Catholic books and magazines are available and that they are read by enough people to keep the publishers in business.

Naturally, this book cannot deal with the question of how to form a cultivated, mentally alert American public. But the basic lines of the answer to the Catholic concern to form spiritually cultivated, alert, and committed Christians (with all that this implies of effort toward human development also) have already been laid out by the confluence of the great movements in the Church today—scriptural, theological, and liturgical. And once the nature of that solution is grasped, it seems so obvious that one is amazed at the long process of research, thought, and experience that has been needed to uncover it. Intellectual effort as such is something few people in any age have much taste for. But every normal human being will make an effort to learn about what really interests him. Consider, for instance, the real scholars of every aspect of baseball to be found at any level of American life. Still more, every human being, even the least intellectual, will make an effort, and not even consider it an effort, to know about *persons* in whom he is interested, whom he himself knows or would like to know. We all seek and absorb a vast amount of information about our friends—their backgrounds, interests, plans, and accomplishments; we read avidly about public personalities who interest us and make great efforts to meet them personally. Nothing else can account for the myriad of movie magazines, sports columns, articles about the families of men prominent in public life, and so on.

This normal human process of coming to know persons and of coming to know *about* them so as to know them better, in the original and truly traditional view, of the Christian life, was meant to be the way in which we come to know Christ. We were meant to learn about Christian truth in all its aspects as related to Him, as a means of coming to know *Him* more fully, and so of deepening our relation with

Him. Of its nature, a deep human relationship includes love, intimacy, and involvement in one another's thoughts, plans, and activities—a growing likeness between the two persons concerned. And so with the "knowledge of Christ" which is made possible for us through the Church; this is why Christ says that His sheep know Him as He knows the Father, and that true life consists in knowing the Father and Jesus Christ whom He has sent.

Every Catholic, then, ought to have made available to him the means to grow in this personal knowledge of Christ and in all the knowledge *about* Christ which will broaden and deepen and fructify this personal knowing of a Person. He should have the basic means of this growth made available to him in the ordinary course of his Catholic life and through whatever other means may suit his particular interests and needs.

These basic means, according to the traditional view of Catholic life that is being rediscovered in our own time, should be given him as he takes part in Catholic worship, above all as he takes part in the Sunday Mass. For here he actually meets Christ who is present "where two or three are gathered together in His Name." Here he hears the inspired words of Scripture in which God speaks to His people, telling them about what He has done for them through His incarnate Son in the past, what He is doing now, what He asks of them, what He promises them. Here the Christian is drawn into Christ's own act of worship and self-giving, made present on the altar. Here he is united more closely with Christ by receiving the Bread which forms us into His Body.

86

All the various means of learning *about* Christ, and about the Christian truth which centers in Him, thus find their place in relation to the personal knowing made possible by Christ's presence and activity in the sacramental acts of the Church and by His speaking to us as human persons through the inspired words of Holy Scripture. All the various "sacred sciences," in fact, have developed through the ages as the result of, and as ancillary to, meditation on Holy Scripture in the context of the life of the Church. Similarly, every individual's grasp of sacred history, doctrine, and the principles of Christian living can be developed from and ordered toward this personal knowing of a Person through the sacraments and Holy Scripture. Some persons will be more capable of an intellectual grasp of Christian truth, some less so; but all can come to love God with their whole minds, according to His commandment.

Moreover, the realization of the relation between knowing Christ and knowing about Christian truth can lead Catholics to participate in the intellectual trends and discoveries of their time. When we begin to realize that we are called to love God with our whole minds, we shall see that this includes the study of His creation in all its manifestations, the study of human nature and human history, the study of all the means of helping human persons toward the full development of their human personalities, as is willed by God. Catholics in the past have been afraid of asking questions; the defensive attitude of the siege has cut us off from modern modes of thought, from facing the questions asked by modern man. But as we begin once more to realize God's call to us through

Christ to know Him, to know about Him, to cultivate and use all our human powers of knowing so as to love and serve Him, then we will no longer be afraid of thought; we will have the basic confidence that God wants us to use our minds, which will enable us to begin to use them for Him.

The traditional Christian view thus brings together thought and religious living, "intellectual" and "spiritual" activity. But the same synthesis also draws all aspects of life into a dynamic relation with Christ. Just as when we come to know another human person intimately we come to share more and more fully in his life, his plans, and his activities, so in coming to know Christ we find ourselves more and more involved in carrying out His work in everything we do. And since the will of Christ is that men "should have life and have it more abundantly," [4] we can begin to see that "Catholic Action," good works, and our own daily work can and should have this same orientation: to help persons in one way or another toward the human and Christian abundance of life offered by Christ. We can begin to see that our participation in the Mass and "Morning Offering" must mean the directing of our whole lives toward achieving Christ's desire "that all may be one" in Him.

The traditional synthesis of "spirituality," thought,

[4] The translation of this phrase given in the *Missel Biblique* (shortly to be published in English by the Liturgical Press, Collegeville, Minnesota), "Je suis venu, moi, pour faire vivre et faire vivre plus intensément"—I have come to make men live and to make them live more intensely—perhaps gives a better notion of its meaning to modern readers than does the usual one.

and activity is thus something quite simple and human, something which can be grasped by anyone in terms of his human experience. It enables each Christian to orient his whole life toward his relationship with Christ. This synthesis makes practical the traditional idea that the whole Christian community is called to grow in the "knowledge of God." If the formation of the whole adult community in the Christian life is what our times require for the effective formation of Catholic young people, it is this traditional way of looking at the Christian life—as an opportunity to grow in the knowledge of Christ, to share His life and work—which must be taught and preached. It is in terms of this view of the Christian life that we must evaluate our present system of education and make our plans for the future.

It is true that, so far, this synthesis has been brought out mainly in works on spirituality.[5] The liturgical movement in this country has, indeed, been seeking from the first to find and express this unity of participation in the sacramental life of the Church, growth in knowledge of Christian truth, and daily life and work.[6] And many of the lay movements of recent years have been feeling their way toward this synthesis, not in theory alone but in practice as well. The Catholic Family Movement, for example, en-

[5] See, for example, Louis Bouyer, *Introduction to Spirituality* (New York: Desclée, 1961); Hans von Balthasar, *Prayer* (New York: Sheed & Ward, 1962); Johannes Pinsk, *Towards the Center of Christian Living* (New York: Herder & Herder, 1961).

[6] See, for example, *The Liturgy and Unity in Christ*, and *Bible, Life and Worship: Proceedings of the 21st and 22nd Liturgical Weeks* (Washington, D. C.: The Liturgical Conference, 1961).

courages its members to come to know Christ in the
Mass and in Holy Scripture and to apply the light
and the motivation thus gained to family and community life. The Young Christian Workers and Students try to apply the same principle in schools,
in offices, and factories. The Grail prepares young
women to exemplify and develop the potentialities of
this synthesis in a many-sided apostolate—helping
young mothers in modern cities, for example, or working as lay missionaries in Africa and South America.
And the oldest of these movements, the Catholic
Worker, under its great leader Dorothy Day, in more
than thirty years of serving society's outcasts, has
shown in word and work that truly coming to know
Christ in the liturgy and in prayer can bring Christians to a loving personal knowledge of their neighbors.

But the explicit, authoritative presentation of this
traditional way of looking at the Christian life by the
teaching Church in this country would bring it to the
ordinary Catholic in the ordinary parish, where it
belongs and is most needed. It would, moreover,
give coherence and effectiveness to the present be-
wildering multiplicity of efforts on the part of individuals and organizations to persuade Catholics to
cultivate some particular exercise or devotion, to take
active part in the Mass, to read the Bible, to read
Catholic books, to take part in study and discussion,
to act along one or another line of Catholic effort, to
give to one or another good work. As things are, the
greater part of this effort still effectively reaches only
a small part of the Catholic population, and does so
as a part-time "extra"; it remains on the margin of

daily life, with little effect on the way in which Catholics conduct their ordinary activities.

In particular, the teaching of the papal encyclicals of the past and present on the need for all Catholics to work for social justice, for racial integration, for the welfare of human beings all over the world, has not yet even faintly affected the way in which the great majority think about current issues or act in their daily lives. Catholics generally have no realization of their religious *duty* to treat every other human being as a person, and so to carry out Christ's command to love one another as He loves us.

But if they were authoritatively and consistently taught and shown that Christ wants to know them as persons in the Church, and that the response He asks for is that they treat others in the same way, then the relation of the love of neighbor to the love of God would begin to be clear to everyone. Then preaching and teaching could bring out the fact that the very complexity of modern society makes all men our next-door neighbors and that Christian love must therefore direct all our thinking and acting in regard to local and world affairs, our whole personal, social, civic, and working lives.

An explicit, authoritative presentation of the traditional idea of the Christian life would, consequently, begin to form Catholics in such a way that they would in turn be motivated to work actively toward their own formation as persons growing in the knowledge of a Person. It would begin to develop the vital adult Catholic life which, as we have seen, is necessary if the formation we now make such efforts to give children is to be truly effective.

Such a return to the traditional idea of the whole Christian community as called to growth in the "knowledge of Christ" would, moreover, render a great service to our whole "child-centered" society. America needs to be awakened to the realization that a mature, responsible adulthood means constant growth and development; the norm is not a fossilized, perpetual youth. American education and the American public, who must support education, desperately need to be convinced that the purpose of schools and colleges and our whole educational setup should be to prepare young people for such maturity, to awaken their own powers of self-development and of free, responsible action. Such a conviction would, in turn, open new possibilities for the fruitful use of leisure time and would lead to the deepened realization of the fundamental truth that "no man is an island."

A return to the traditional idea of the Christian life would, of course, find much to overcome in American Catholicism. But it would discover that it had more than a little to build on—most important, perhaps, the almost universal desire to find a dynamic pattern that gives meaning and dignity to daily life. And in the work of the Council and of the late Pope John XXIII—the work being carried on by Pope Paul VI—we find that precisely such a response to the present situation is being encouraged and set in motion. In answering the call to renew Catholic life along the lines being indicated by the Council, shall we not find the solution to the problem of the religious formation of the Catholic community as a whole? The following chapter will be devoted to a further examination of this possibility.

5

NEW
VISTAS

No ONE doubts that the situation of Catholics in this country and the situation of the Church in relation to our society have changed greatly since the nineteenth century. The typical Catholic is no longer a bewildered immigrant, strange to American ways and often speaking a language other than English. He is an established member of American society, more and more likely to be a college graduate, pursuing a career in business or one of the professions. The sweeping change that has occurred is illustrated by the remark made by a professor in one of the major seminaries, that when he was a student, seminarians came mainly from unskilled or semiskilled backgrounds, whereas now the great majority have fathers engaged in professional work.

This means, on the one hand, that the clergy are no longer the only educated Catholic group and, on the other, that much more can be expected of a great many of the laity in the way of informed, mature, responsible cooperation in the thought and work of the Church. Some of the laity, at least, are aware of this and eager to take such a part. A survey of Catholics' attitudes to questions likely to be discussed at the Second Vatican Council was recently conducted by the magazine *Eucharist* in cooperation with some twenty diocesan papers. These papers, which have a combined circulation of 500,000 scattered throughout the country, with the greatest concentration in the Midwest and Southwest, printed a questionnaire which respondents were asked to fill in and send to *Eucharist*. More than 2,000 replies were received, 65 per cent from Catholics with a college education.

Of those answering the questionnaire, 97 per cent wanted more effective guidance in understanding and living the liturgy; 88 per cent wanted greater emphasis on, and instruction in, the Bible; 92 per cent, more emphasis on the universal spirituality of the Church and less on particular devotions; 84 per cent asked that a greater consultative voice be given the laity in Church and school administration; 89 per cent mentioned the need for better channels of communication between the laity and the hierarchy; 48 per cent felt that the laity are as of now poorly prepared for a more active role in the Church; 92 per cent wanted it made clear that, once the essentials are safeguarded, the Church is ready to make every possible change that would improve the prospects of unity among Christians.[1]

[1] *Eucharist*, October, 1962, pp. 33-40. The percentage of those responding to this questionnaire—25 per cent—may not seem very impressive, but the normal expectation for a newspaper survey with no prizes or "gimmicks" is only about 1 or 2 per cent. The fact should also be taken into account that not all who subscribe to diocesan newapers read them carefully. This percentage, then, is

At least a representative number of lay Catholics, therefore, are ready for a change. They want a religious life centered in the liturgy and Scripture; they want a greater share in the life and work of the Church; they want an end to defensiveness; they want the possibility of "dialogue" with those of other faiths.

While the composition of the Catholic Church in America has thus altered in the last hundred years, so has the way it is regarded by those of different faiths, as well as the way Catholics think about others. The "Roman Church" no longer seems something strange and foreign, fearfully regarded by Protestants as the "Scarlet Woman." Distrust of the "monolithic" Church of Rome still exists, but many Protestants are eager for true tolerance and greater exchange—an attitude which the Council and the way in which the Protestant observers there have been treated have enormously strengthened. Even a few years ago, what Protestant or Catholic could have imagined a Cardinal of the Roman Church—and a foreigner at that —giving a series of talks on the reunion of Christians under the auspices of the Harvard Divinity School, such as took place at the Roman Catholic–Protestant Colloquium held in March 1963? Or a lecture on a Council of the Catholic Church given by a Protestant minister under both Catholic and Protestant auspices, illustrated with slides he had taken at the

somewhat more significant than might appear at first sight. In any case, it indicates that among the readers sufficiently interested in the questions to be discussed at the Council to fill out, cut out, and mail in a questionnaire, the great majority favored the aims of the renewal.

Council, and attended by both Catholics and Protestants?

Modern Scripture study is drawing Protestant and Catholic scholars together. One member of a discussion group composed of scholars of both faiths recently noted that the unanimity of the experts as to the literal sense of any text was found to be so complete that the presence of both a Catholic and a Protestant expert was unnecessary—either one could rely on the other to deal with whatever questions arose. The rise of a liturgical movement in Protestantism as well as in Catholicism is providing another basis for positive exchange. The recent conference on religion and race, at which representatives of all the major religious groups met to plan a common struggle against the evil of racial segregation, points to similar hopes.

The Roman Catholic Church, then, is certainly not under siege from Protestantism. We no longer need to learn Catholic teaching "against" Protestantism. We need, on the contrary, to become aware of how much Catholics and the various Protestant groups have in common, at the same time discovering just where—and the historical reasons why—we differ.[2]

A similar effort to eliminate prejudice and foster

[2] Cardinal Bea, speaking at Boston College on March 26, 1963, "called upon all Christians to assume the serious duty and privilege of participating in the promotion of Christian unity. . . . Addressing his remarks especially to the students, the Cardinal said that the 'serious duty and privilege' of involvement in the work of Christian unity implies an understanding of the means and aims of the ecumenical movement and, especially, what means are at the disposal of all Christians to promote unity." *The Pilot*, Boston, Massachusetts, March 30, 1963.

real communication has at least been initiated with the Jews. Christians, both Protestant and Catholic, have begun to examine their popular preaching, teaching, liturgical formulas, and theological treatises to see where we have misrepresented the true New Testament doctrine concerning the Jews. Various publications are directed to discussing these questions on various levels, including the popular one, and to foster a truly Christian love for our Jewish neighbors.[3]

At the same time, the temper of society in general with regard to religion has changed a great deal. In the nineteenth century and the early decades of the twentieth, people generally were very much concerned about whether there was a God, and, if there was, what He expected of men. Protestants quarreled with one another on details of belief and practice; all of them "protested" against the Catholic Church; even deists, as well as militant atheists, tried to impose their views on others.

But today things are different. Few of the millions who do not believe in God bother to try to prove His nonexistence; they take it for granted. God is not attacked, He is simply ignored. Modern "secular humanism" [4] may be called a religion in the sense that it determines the outlook of many people on

[3] See "The Ecumenical Movement and the Jews," *The Ecumenist,* I, 3, pp. 36ff.; also Gregory Baum, *The Jews and the Gospel* (Westminster, Md.: The Newman Press, 1961).

[4] The term is used here in the sense defined earlier, as meaning the generally anthropocentric climate of our day, not the positive "religion" of some group suspected of a determination to eliminate traditional religion from American life.

life, but it is not a religion in the sense of offering any sort of link between man and God. Its whole ethos is precisely to be concerned with man and not with God.

A large proportion of Americans do certainly profess some sort of belief in God, and church membership is higher than ever before. Many people are seriously concerned lest, in the public schools and in public life, God's existence as the Supreme Being and the source of blessings to men should no longer be formally acknowledged. But most of the discussions about prayer in the public schools—witness the arguments presented before the Supreme Court— argue that such a practice is part of our "religious heritage," and that it favors order and morality—both "man-centered" arguments. And many popular books and articles on religious subjects indicate that God is thought of primarily as a bulwark against disaster and Communism, an aid to the "good guys" in achieving their own ends—as in *God Is My Co-Pilot* or *The Man Upstairs*.

Religious beliefs, then, are not besieged by today's secular humanism, but they are in danger of being tainted by its secularism. It is not an attacking army fighting the churches on the level of intellectual conviction or even of religious practice. We need, in fact, very carefully to distinguish the humanistic from the secularistic trends in today's mentality, identifying ourselves as far as possible in thought and action with the former while endeavoring to purge ourselves of the latter. Today's secularism has an insidious tendency to turn religion itself manwards, to put God at the service of man, rather than man at the service of

God. But today's humanistic tendencies call out to true religion for cooperation and fulfillment. They demand that Christians show precisely how God's transforming love is concerned with human persons, with human values, with human society and progress, and how it can give human strivings their fullest possible meaning.

In the climate of secular humanism, Christians can no longer be uninterested in religion and continue for long to lead religious lives. But neither can they be uninterested in the concerns of their neighbor or in their society's turmoil of conflicting interests and still fulfill the demands of the Christian vocation. Do we really believe that God is effectively intervening in human life, in our own lives? Are we so vitally interested in Him that we want to encounter Him and come to know Him better day by day as He makes Himself available to us in the Church? Are we so vitally concerned about His plan for mankind that we are willing to commit ourselves and our whole lives to carrying it out in our world? If so, how can we evade a full commitment to humanism, and to expanding the horizons of human life beyond humanism toward those that God has opened out in His love? Here is the challenge that secular humanism offers us today.

It is no disloyalty to the Church to say that the mentality of the past, the mentality of the siege, is not able to meet this new challenge. Carried into the present context, the old mentality has in fact come so close to that of secularism that to slip from one to another is only too easy. If you believe that God's only concern with human life is to help you save your soul in the hereafter, it is very difficult to be interested in Him here and now except during times of crisis. ("There are no atheists in foxholes," as was so often said during World War II.) So long as you do not positively deny Catholic doctrine or disobey the Commandments, you are safe. . . . God has little part in your daily life and its concerns, so little that when it comes to a real conflict between His claims and those of daily life, it would take a miracle of grace to make His claims paramount. Consequently, even well-instructed Catholics slide away from the Church, rather than leave it deliberately, in the vague hope that God won't really mind and will save them in the end.

At the same time, the old mentality does not see human values as included in the scope of Christ's redeeming work. As has been noted in the previous chapter, Catholics generally feel no religious necessity to carry out their daily work as a service of love to their neighbor; to fight segregation; to engage in the reform of the social and economic orders; to involve themselves in efforts toward peace. The old mentality has, consequently, tended to cut Catholics off from what is truly humanistic in today's world, while it has allowed them too easily to become submerged in its secularism.

Another result has been that, in the minds of many Catholics, religion has been increasingly dissociated from the real concerns of their lives. It has seemed to have nothing constructive to say or suggest about daily work, about the agonizing difficulties of Christian married life in modern society, about today's vast sociological and economic problems, about modern warfare, about anything that really concerns modern man. Some Catholics are quite content with this dissociation; thinking of religion primarily as the business of priests and religious, they tend to feel resentful now that the Church is beginning to "interfere" with social and economic life by laying down principles and suggesting lines of action, as Pope John XXIII did in *Mater et Magistra* and *Pacem in Terris*. On the other hand, an increasing number are beginning to feel that a religion which is merely a Sunday affair, a matter of habit and social conformity or private devotion, is not really religion at all. Consequently one cannot help wondering how long, if the old mentality should continue to dominate, the practice of religion would continue among the intelligent and truly religious members of the coming generation.

It seems providential, then, that the new spirit which has been growing up in the Church in recent decades—a spirit which the first session of the Council showed to be that of the majority of the assembled Fathers—should be directed precisely toward bringing Christ's truth and life once more *into* human life, toward bringing human life once more into dynamic relation with God's plan of salvation.

Our religion has appeared to be kept tidily apart from life, crystallized in abstract formulas and pious sentiments, of concern only to individuals and entailing only optional "good works." Now it is becoming clear that we each are to take our own part in the vast and many-sided work of making Christ's message and Christ's work once more seem relevant to modern thought, to modern problems, to modern life, and to modern persons. Pope John XXIII, in calling the Council, summoned the authorities and theologians of the Church to inaugurate the work of restating Christ's unchanging message in terms truly intelligible to modern man. If this message is actually to reach our neighbors, every Catholic will eventually need to make an effort of his own to think in these terms. Again, we have all been called, as has been noted, to cooperate in the promotion of Christian unity. And in the encyclical *Pacem in Terris,* Pope John XXIII called on all Catholics to realize that every human being is a person, to be treated as such; he called on us to cooperate with men of good will and with all hopeful tendencies of our times to promote true human welfare and development.

But, as the late Pope said very explicitly, this will require bringing the light and love of Christ into daily life and work; it will require personal integration of our religious life and our activities in the world of men:

Once again we deem it opportune to remind our children of their duty to take an active part in public life, and to contribute toward the attainment of the common good of the entire human family as well as to that of their own political community. They should endeavor therefore in the light of the faith and with the strength of love, to insure that the various institutions—whether economic, social, cultural, or political in purpose— should be such as not to create obstacles, but rather to facilitate or render less arduous man's perfecting of him-

self both in the natural order as well as in the supernatural.

He went on to say that faith and good will are not
enough; to work effectively toward these ends, one
must be "scientifically competent, technically capable
and skilled in the practice of his profession."

This, equally, is not enough by itself; there must be
integration between faith and charity on the one hand
and technical competence on the other.

It is certainly necessary that human beings carry on their
own temporal activities in accordance with the laws
governing them and following the methods correspond-
ing to their nature. But at the same time it is also necessary that they should carry on their activities as acts
within the moral order; therefore, as the exercise or vin-
dication of right, as the fulfillment of duty or the per-
formance of service, as a positive answer to the providential design of God directed to salvation. . . . It is necessary therefore [for Christians] that the interior unity [of
religious belief and action in the temporal sphere] be
re-established, and that in their temporal activity faith
should be present as a beacon to give light, and charity
as a force to give life.

This unity stressed by the late Pope means above
all that Catholics must realize afresh their vocation
as instruments of Christ's love; it means that they
must realize anew His presence and activity in *their*
lives; it means that they must be able to make more
immediate contact with Him as He reveals and gives

Himself to them in the Church. The response of the Church to today's secular humanism must above all be a "sacramental" one. We must realize afresh, that is, that Christ is the supreme sacrament of God's love, the effective sign of God's intervention in human history and human life; that He continues to witness to God's love for mankind and to communicate it to men above all in the sacramental life of the Chuch, thus enabling Christians to be effective signs of this love among their fellow men.

This is why a great part of the work of the Council as envisaged in the opening address by the Pope is the reform of institutions and practices so that the presence and activity of Christ in the Church will be more immediately evident and available to the faithful. And this is also why the first step taken by the Council was to consider a Constitution on the Liturgy. The section of that Constitution accepted at the 1962 session restates the traditional idea of God's plan for the salvation of mankind; it places the sacramental life of the Church, centered in the celebration of the Eucharist, at the heart of the whole life and work of the Church and of each individual Catholic. It sets up principles for a reform of the sacramental rites which will facilitate that refocusing.[5]

[5] "It was not by chance that the first schema to be considered was on the sacred liturgy which defines the relationship between man and God. Since it is the highest form of relationship, it must be based on the solid foundation of revelation and the apostolic preaching. . . ." (Pope John XXIII, at the closing session of the Council.)

"The Council's overwhelming acceptance of the first chapter of the schema on liturgy was a truly revolutionary step, though the fact is only slowly beginning to dawn on observers here. An article

For a change in our attitude to the Christian life is bound up with a change in our attitude to the sacraments, and a reform of the sacramental rites is necessary to bring this change about. And all three are necessary if we are to carry out our Christian vocation in today's world.

The way in which the outlook of the siege narrowed down the idea of God's redemptive purpose to that of saving our souls has already been described. But the traditional idea, as restated in the document accepted by the Council, is that Christ was sent by the Father to give us *His* life, to communicate to us God's Spirit, to give us the amazing dignity and privilege of sharing in Christ's worship of the Father and His work for mankind, and so to achieve a purpose beyond ourselves.

Again, the old outlook saw the sacraments and prayer as "means of grace" to be used by each person for his own needs. The genuinely traditional outlook sees the sacraments as the chief acts of Christ in the Church through which He reveals Himself to us, gives us His life, forms us to its requirements, draws us into the current of His self-giving to the Father and to men, and unites us with one another in the Spirit of love. The sacraments are, in short, privileged occasions of our meeting with Christ and coming to know Him in the fullest possible sense.

by the noted Benedictine professor of liturgy, Dom Cyprian Vagaggini, published in *L'Osservatore Romano* for December 8, spells out the significance of the principles established in this conciliar document. The Church's sacramental and prayer life is now acknowledged to be at the very heart of her activities. It is the substance of the Catholic faith in action." (Xavier Rynne, *op. cit.,* p. 252.)

This is why the celebration of the sacraments must be focal in the life of the Church and of each Christian. To see them in any other way would be as though, in a human relationship, one thought of one's meetings with a friend as less important than receiving his messages indirectly, reading about him or talking about him with other people.

And this is why active participation in the Mass and the other sacramental celebrations is so clearly necessary. We come to know another person by really listening to what he says to us, not by thinking about something else—even about something connected with him—when he is speaking. So at Mass, for instance, we need really to be aware of the sacramental rites themselves as communicating to us the mind of Christ.

Again, in a meeting with a human friend, we not only listen, we respond to what he says to us. If he suggests some action in common, we eagerly take part in it with him. So at the Mass and the other sacraments, we need to respond to God's Word with the welcome of faith and with prayer; we need to respond to Christ's invitation to join with Him in His great act of worship, His Eucharistic sacrifice; we need to commit ourselves with Him to making our whole lives an offering of praise to God and a loving service of men.

And finally, if the meeting with one's friend is not only a matter of intimate communication between two persons but also of a whole group of persons united by affection for a common friend, then our listening and responding to him, our joining in his action, is a personal and also a communal affair—

the more personal for being communal. And so at Mass. As we come to know Christ more intimately, we come to know one another in Him. As we share His life and activity more fully, we share those of one another as well. The Mass and the other sacramental actions of the Church, consequently, are in themselves community actions which unite us with one another the more closely because of our union with Christ.

But the liturgy itself also needs reforming if Catholics are to know Christ by taking part in it. The idea that the liturgy could mean all this to ordinary Catholics today cannot but seem unrealistic if we think of it as it is still too often carried out: a distant priest muttering an incomprehensible language before the altar and going through rites in which—no matter how elaborate or "colorful" they may be—the congregation apparently has no part. The proposal may seem less unrealistic, although still, perhaps, not entirely convincing, to anyone who has taken part in a Mass celebrated as comprehensibly and giving the people as full a part as is possible under the present regulations.

For this reason the Constitution on the Liturgy has laid down principles for making the needed changes. The first aim of the reform is to ensure that the sacramental signs really signify to modern people what they are meant to signify. For the liturgy is essentially a complex of sacred signs, intended not only to "effect what they signify" but also to "signify what they effect." These signs are essentially scriptural, both in form and content. Shaped and permeated by God's inspired Word, they are meant to be "words," communications of the Incarnate Word here present and active in His Church. Their function is precisely to open out to us the meaning of what Christ is doing for us here and now in the context of the whole history of salvation, and to give us concrete ways of responding to that message and that action. But through the centuries, the pristine simplicity of those signs has been overlaid and obscured; they have ceased really to communicate Christ's message to us even though they do of course continue to communicate His grace. Thus the reform that is to be initiated is expected to make use of modern languages, as well as to simplify and clarify the rites themselves and, in certain nonessentials, adapt them to the needs of particular cultures.

A second aim of the reform will be to bring out through the structure of the rites the fact that the liturgy is truly the action of the Christian community in which everyone present has an active part, both outwardly and inwardly. The rites were designed in this way in the first place; but through the course of centuries all the parts in a low Mass were taken over by the priest and his servers, and those in a high Mass by the priest, the sacred ministers, and the choir. Now the people are once again to have their proper external part, expressing, fostering, and completing their interior participation. And all the other participants are to take their own parts and not to duplicate one another's (for instance, the celebrant will not have to read a Lesson to himself while it is being publicly proclaimed by a lector).

No one, of course, can easily imagine what the Mass (or any other sacramental celebration) will actually be like when the rites have been reformed, *and* when our whole way of thinking about and living the Christian life has also been changed from the static to the dynamic; from the intellectualist and mechanical to the personal; from the individualistic to the communal; from the a-historical to the existential; from the passive and analytic to the appreciative and active; when everyone who takes part is aware of the commitment to God's love and to the achievement of His purposes in human history which His participation implies.

The "active participation" of recent years has had to contend not only with the difficulties posed by the present rites, but also with an outlook to which such participation is fundamentally alien. Thus it has often seemed to be sterile, to have no effect on Catholic living—to be merely something new for the people to do at Mass. The active participation of the future will be another matter entirely. Not only will the rites call for it and facilitate it, but—even more important—it will be carried out by persons aware of, and thus potentially responsive to, Christ's desire to involve them here and now in His action and His life.

We can see that when the Mass and the other sacramental acts of the Church are celebrated in such a way, they will really be formative, that the faithful who truly take part in them will grow in the knowledge of Christ. They will have the attitude that makes possible "learning by doing"; they will be formed in the spirit and pattern of Christian prayer through hearing and responding to what Holy Scripture tells them of God. They will be formed in the spirit of self-giving love by taking part in Christ's Eucharist. Moreover, the Scriptural readings at the Mass and at other rites will really communicate Christ's revelation of Himself and of the Father. The sermons given at Mass and during other sacramental rites can then further unfold to a particular congregation the meaning of the Bible and the liturgy in relation to Christ's present sacramental action and to their own lives.[6]

Consequently, the idea that the central formative force in the Catholic life of the future should be participation in the Mass, Sunday by Sunday, year by year, no longer appears unrealistic. And it begins to seem even more of a practical possibility in view of the fact that all other forms of religious instruction and formation are to be oriented toward more appreciative and wholehearted participation in the sacred rites. The document on the liturgy approved by the Council indicates that everything in the Christian life—prayer, suffering, and the carrying out of our daily activities—is to be understood as flowing toward and from this participation and that all instruction in Christian truth is to bring out this integration.

This approach is understood as applicable on every

---

[6] See *The Liturgy and the Word of God* (Collegeville, Minnesota: Liturgical Press, 1958). Many people suppose that a more meaningful Mass would have to be a longer one, and wonder how this could be practicable in parishes with an already crowded Mass schedule—or a parking problem. As a matter of fact, the projected reform will be toward simplification (even though expansion will be possible in cultures that desire it); a fear of impractically long services in the future is therefore quite unnecessary.

level. The document recommends even to seminary "professors of other theological subjects, especially of dogma, spiritual theology and pastoral theology, that they bring out so clearly . . . the mystery of Christ and the history of salvation that the relation of each subject to the liturgy is immediately evident, and thus a considerable contribution will be made to the work of priestly formation." The consensus of the teaching authorities of the Church, therefore, indicates that we are to rethink the problem of Catholic formation in these terms.

To anyone who begins to do so, it becomes evident that the first objective must be the arousing of each person's interest and enthusiasm, leading to his own active cooperation in the formative work of Christ and the Holy Spirit. The purpose of instruction in Christian doctrine will no longer be merely to make sure, on the lower levels, that exact formulas are memorized or, on the higher, that a merely intellectual grasp of doctrine has been gained. Exact formulations will still have their place—but only as useful summaries of realities that are first to be grasped in the living context of God's scriptural Word addressed to us here and now, of God's action in our regard here and now, and of our response to that action in daily life.

Again, instruction in morals and Christian living will need to return to the perspectives of the New Testament, showing that we are to become humble, nonacquisitive, chaste, temperate, and courageous because we are members of Christ, called and enabled to "live and walk in the Spirit." We are to love with the generous love that seeks the good of the other because in the sacraments we are given the Spirit of God's own infinite generosity. Everything that we do is to be ordered to the praise of God in Christ here and now, and to the preparation of ourselves and mankind for His ultimate return.

Finally, the new outlook requires that formation in prayer, in morals, and in the practice of the Christian life must go beyond the level of the "superego," to use the Freudian expression—that is, the pressure of the need to do what is expected by others, and of the feeling of guilt if one does not. Christians are to be formed to the freedom of the Spirit, to the free obedience of children of God, who obey His law of love freely and intelligently, as their own law, formed from within by the Spirit and taught from without by the Church—a law which only a continuing co-operation with the Holy Spirit can interpret in detail and apply concretely in daily life.

This, then, is the kind of instruction we need to plan for—one by its very nature centered in the Church, rather than in the school, and calling for personal thought and effort rather than "indoctrination." It will therefore be the work of the pastor, the parent, and the "coach" in Christian living rather than that simply of the classroom teacher. And it is in relation to the aim of making such instruction and formation available to all Catholics that we need to evaluate our present means of instruction and our Catholic school system as a whole.

The situation of the American Catholic today may be summarized as follows: Whereas he was once imprisoned in the mentality of the siege, he need be so no longer. The spirit of ecumenism is freeing him of the fear of denominational hostility. And although he now faces the danger of secularism, he finds this very secularism so interwoven with genuine humanism as to call for the active presence of Christians in modern society.

Threats from without, therefore, need no longer condition his thinking or behavior. What he must now face is, rather, the need for setting himself in order from within—a conscious shift from a defensive and minimal Christianity to that fullness of life which Christ came to give him, and which he is to share with his neighbors. With all his fellow members of the Church he must, consequently, learn how to participate as a co-worker with Christ in both work and worship. What is needed, therefore, is a formation aimed toward these supreme ends, a formation not diverted, as it so largely is today, toward other secondary ends. And what is needed to make this possible is hardly less than a revolution in Catholic education and Catholic life.

6

FEARS—
REALISTIC
AND
OTHERWISE

IN THINKING about the whole question of religious education in the light of the Council, we must obviously consider that if the "new" outlook is to be communicated to the entire Catholic body—priests, religious, and laity—a great and unusual effort will have to be made. Before we discuss this problem, however, it may be well to take a look at the fears, both those that are explicit and those that are more or less hidden, which many of us are likely to entertain concerning the open, sacramental Catholicism proposed and diffused by the Council.

Our religious attitudes are naturally bound up with our earliest and most cherished associations. To accept any suggestion that they could be improved upon may therefore sometimes appear rather like a betrayal of loyalties, criticism of the holiest and dearest persons we have known—persons who lived and died in the piety of the old outlook, and who trained us to be devout in the same way. Nevertheless, the answer to these fears is so clear as to be indisputable, if not always easy to apply. Can there be any doubt that true loyalty to the past consists not merely in retaining what was good in it, but also in being willing to go ahead, to grow out of what was partial and static? And would not our devout elders themselves have done precisely this, had they been living today?

In the same way, religious attitudes are naturally interwoven with the deepest roots of our emotional life; to change them seems to threaten our deepest security, the security of our very relation with God— all the more since to so many Catholics their religion has meant security above all, eternal security in return for living and doing rightly, and the consolations offered by religion to those who suffer and are tried by life here and now. The new attitude may appear as a threat to all this. There may be the fear that if we change our accustomed ways of praying, we shall be deprived of the familiar sense of safety those ways afforded us. Again, "active" participation in worship may seem to bring in the outside world of human activity precisely where we have been glad to leave it behind. And, in the same way, the idea that all of daily life should be positively formed by our religious ideas and attitudes may seem to make prayer something less special and sacred, less set apart from the untidy turmoil of ordinary life.

Such fears of losing one's personal sense of the holy should certainly not be minimized; rather, they must be looked at carefully—and when that is done, they may be found to have been needless. The new outlook is guaranteed to be traditional in the deepest sense, to be truly in accord with God's plan, by consensus of the highest authorities of the Church. It opens out the possibility of a greater personal intimacy with Christ, the intimacy of fellow workers. We shall, therefore, be more secure, not less, and find deeper consolation, not confusion, in working to make this outlook our own.

Lay Catholics generally have tended to think of religion as a part of life, but a part they are quite content to leave mainly to the clergy. Such persons may shrink from the responsibility of making themselves religiously, as well as humanly, competent in all the areas of their daily lives. To this attitude there can be only one answer—namely, the realization that we are *all* asked to cooperate with the light and grace of Christ and of the Holy Spirit; that we are *all* expected to come to know Christ and so to know His will for our own individual lives, even though we are not all required to be experts in formal theology; that it is the obligation of *all* of us to become familiar with the teachings of the Church on social justice, even though we are not all required to become specialists in casuistry or canon law; and that *each* of us is called upon to try to carry out all this in his ordinary area of competence, whether or not he always succeeds perfectly in the attempt.

Again, many laymen are accustomed to thinking of the Cross as meaning no more than the patient endurance of physical and mental suffering, and the occasional voluntary "sacrifice" of this or that legitimate pleasure—for example, during Lent. Never having realized the implications of their baptism, they cannot help being dismayed at a view of the Christian life which makes the daily dying to oneself, the effort to spend oneself ever more fully for God and men, an integral part of his Christian commitment.

It is already evident that many Catholics also have an unconscious fear of damage to their present status if they were to take the papal encyclicals seriously— and what the new outlook means is that every Catholic *must* take them seriously. The Church and Catholics generally have now managed to achieve a secure and even a comfortable place in our society. But if we all begin to see it as our religious duty to work with other men of good will in carrying out the principles of *Mater et Magistra* and *Pacem in Terris,* the Church and her members are bound to come into conflict with those interests which, directly or indirectly, foster injustice and dehumanization. Anyone who really tries to spread the "fire on the earth" that Christ enkindled cannot expect to be in conformity with everything that now is advertised as the "American way of life."

Such fears have a very real foundation. The only answer that can be made to them is the anwer our very faith requires us to make: that if the effort toward continual self-giving is now clearly required of every Catholic, if the effort to implement papal social teachings is no longer optional but obligatory, then the serious Catholic will be given grace to make that effort in response to Christ's invitation.

Among pastors, parents, and teachers, fears of a quite different kind are likely to arise. There will be some who cannot help fearing the risks involved in substituting for the clearly defined objective of inculcating basic Catholic beliefs and practices the seemingly indefinite aim of awakening, enlightening, and sustaining personal effort to know Christ and to fulfill His requirements. Will children so brought up, it may be asked, really know their faith? If the old

117

bulwarks are removed—conformity to a group, habits established below the level of conscious intention— how many ordinary Catholics will be able to stand up against the pressures of secular society? How many will retain Christian moral standards and continue to practice their faith? Is it realistic to expect any ordinary child or adult to be interested in religion—interested enough to work at it and even to suffer for it?

The most profound answer to these fears is, certainly, that God's plan for our salvation in Christ, by its very nature calls for a free response to God's love in cooperation with His grace; new implications of this truth are now being brought out in the Church. We cannot ultimately go wrong, therefore, whatever the apparent risks, in working in accordance with God's design. And, obviously, our relations with God must be intrinsically interesting, the most interesting realities in our lives. It was the old outlook that made religion seem dull—by divorcing it from the real concerns of ordinary people, by separating all but its devotional aspects from the deep human desire to know a Person. It is not God who makes religion uninteresting, but the way in which religion is presented. It may take a long time and much effort to overcome this difficulty, especially in older people; nevertheless, the effort must be made. For children never find religion dull until someone has made it seem so. And so until their elders begin to find it interesting, there is little use in trying to start afresh with a new generation.

Thus laymen have their own fears concerning the effects of the new outlook, and some of these may be shared by members of the clergy. But for priests there will be still other fears peculiar to themselves. The layman, after all, has much to gain in place of the familiar, the routine, the narrowly secure view of religion. The new outlook invests him and his life with a new dignity and a new interest; it gives meaning and purpose to his daily existence. But priests may well feel that they will lose not only much that the layman fears to lose, but a great deal more.

The old outlook has, after all, been very deeply ingrained in our priests by their training; they have lived their whole priestly lives and carried out their priestly work in accordance with it. Whether a priest has had the whole or only a part of his preliminary education in a Catholic school, he has almost invariably received his priestly formation in a seminary which was itself imbued with the mentality of the siege. After all, the present seminary setup was established during the Counter Reformation. American seminaries were first being founded while anti-Catholic prejudice ran high. In fact, professors who trained the most senior of the present older clergy could look back on the days of real anti-Catholic violence, the days of the Know-Nothings and the Ku Klux Klan.

Moreover, the senior clergy themselves—and this means the majority of seminary professors—came from immigrant families of low economic and social status. (Cardinal Cushing, for example, has been quoted as saying that some twenty-five years ago there were no bishops whose parents had gone to college.) The older clergy, then, including those who set the general tone in seminaries, were brought up in the mentality of an out-group; and it cannot but be difficult for members of such a group to shift from a defensive way of looking at things. This means that the great majority of the leaders of the American Church, both national and local, are wedded by their whole tradition to the mentality of the siege, and also that up to the present time, that mentality has been more or less prominent in the formation of priests.

In addition, the present educational situation has to a certain degree revived the old feeling that the Church in America is facing an antagonistic state and that Catholics in America are opposed by hostile groups intent on depriving them of their rights as citizens. Among many of the clergy the current attempt to show the justice of federal aid to Catholic schools has reawakened the dormant belief that there are forces in American society determined to undermine the Church and to wean Catholics away from their faith. The effect of all this has been to cause many priests to cling more closely than ever before to the mentality of the siege, with all that it implies, and to the school system as both the focus and the crown of American Catholic life.

Further, the combination of seminary training and the discipline of the priestly life itself tends to produce—even more strongly than, say, the combination of West Point training and army life—a group of men with a strong *esprit de corps,* formed and dedicated to a particular way of looking at and doing things. Any suggestion that there might be deficiencies in the mentality in which they were formed and in accordance with which they have carried out their life work may well seem to be a radical criticism of the Church itself and of their own priestly efforts. For if army or navy personnel are likely to be conservative, how much more so a priest, since not only his calling but his religious dedication to that calling is involved? And of course the very fact that the old outlook is by nature defensive can easily make resistance against the infiltration of new ideas seem a positive duty. All this helps to explain why the great majority of the clergy of the United States have been hesitant about welcoming or fostering new trends in the life of the Church.

In addition, it should be remembered that none of the great upheavals by which Europe in this century has been so deeply shaken have had the same effect in America. Our priests have not had to face mass defections from the Church or the impact of Communism; our society has not confronted them with any obvious reasons or any clear-cut demand for a radical change in the Church's approach to modern human problems. They still, in great part, are lulled by figures on attendance at Mass and the reception of the sacraments, and can easily believe that all is well with things as they are. Moreover, as has frequently been pointed out, they have been too busy building up the Church materially to have much time or inclination for keeping in touch with recent Catholic thought or to be aware of the solid work of scholarship behind the modern trends.

Thus the present ironic situation has arisen: It is precisely those charged with the mission of leading the faithful to the "primary and indispensable source of the true Christian spirit" who have the most difficulty in recognizing that source for what it is.

One of the characteristics of the old mentality was its preoccupation with the *ex opere operato* ("from the work's having been carried out") aspect of the sacraments—the fact that when they are carried out as the Church prescribes, by an authorized person, they necessarily produce their essential effects so long as no insuperable obstacle intervenes. This doctrine is a very useful clarification of the truth that Christ acts through the sacraments regardless of the fitness or unfitness of His human minister, and with the *necessity* only for the very minimum of willingness on the part of the recipient (and none at all on the part of infants). But through the centuries, in conjunction with many other factors—some of which have been brought out in Chapter Three—an almost exclusive emphasis on this aspect has led to regarding the sacraments as a kind of machinery set up by Christ to provide a commodity called grace, which is needed in order to live rightly and to get to heaven. Indeed, a favorite figure of speech, used with variations in many sermons, is that the faithful should receive Communion frequently in order to be "filled up with grace."

Priests consequently think of themselves as those appointed and empowered by Christ to provide the sacraments to passive recipients. Celebrating the Mass and administering the sacraments are the priest's duty and privilege; the laity need only take care to avail themselves of these means of grace at the appropriate times. Moreover, providing Mass and the sacraments seems like only one pastoral duty out of many—even though offering "his" Mass is regarded as the supreme privilege, so far as the priest himself is concerned.

It requires an extraordinary mental revolution—

one might almost say a "conversion," and there are priests who have used the word in this connection— for a priest to think of Mass and the sacraments as the acts of Christ through which He wills to communicate with His people and to involve them in His activity, and to think of celebrating the sacraments so as most fully to involve the faithful and help them to respond to Christ's action as the focus of all his pastoral activity. Practically speaking, quite apart from any suggested changes in the rites, for a priest to begin to celebrate Mass so that the people can take part in it, for him to be aware of their presence and activity as a vital part of the total celebration, means a change in his ingrained way of celebrating. And to many, the possibility of such a change is deeply disturbing.

Again, many a priest is accustomed to thinking of religion as his "occupation" as distinct from that of the laity. The idea that the ordinary layman is meant to be vitally interested in religion can be even a little horrifying, since the laymen he meets who evidence any unusual concern about religious matters are frequently more or less unbalanced, if not out-and-out fanatics. And, too, there may be the unconscious feeling that if every Catholic were to become as religious-minded in his daily life as a priest or a nun is called upon to be by his or her specially consecrated vocation, a devaluation of the priestly or the religious dedication would somehow result.

Many priests and religious also fear that the spread of the ideas that every Catholic has a vocation to serve God and his neighbor in some special way, and that there is a Christian vocation underlying all particular vocations, will lessen the attraction of the priestly and religious life for young people. Actually, there is good reason to believe that the opposite may prove true. When all young Catholics are shown that the Christian life must involve self-sacrifice, even heroism—that it is not a question of choosing between an easier but less supernaturally secure life as a layman and a more difficult but more certain way of life as a priest or religious, we may well have not fewer but more priestly and religious vocations. And as the priestly life appears to be more clearly what it is—not primarily that of an administrator but that of a pastor—more young men might well be drawn to it.

What is especially needed to allay all these fears is for our bishops to communicate to their priests the full implications of the pastoral office which they themselves have drawn from the Council. As has often been pointed out, this Council was not called *against* anything, but in order to bring about a renewal of Catholic life. The bishops convened in the Council, therefore, could come to see themselves as shepherds, instruments of the One Shepherd, called not only to defend His flock against ravening wolves but also to lead it to the pastures of life. Pope John XXIII said repeatedly that the aims of the Council were to be pastoral, oriented toward the more effective *cura animarum*—a phrase unfortunately translated as "the care of souls" and taken to mean primarily a protective care, but actually meaning the care of *persons,* the positive concern to bring Christ's message and life to persons, to remove obstacles to their meeting with Christ. If all priests could now come to share this view of their pastoral dignity and office—if they could come to see that it adds to the priestly dignity and privilege rather than detracts from it—one of the chief obstacles in the way of priests' gaining the outlook of the renewal would be removed.

The same deeper, more positive view of the pastoral office will also enable priests to lay aside the feeling that it is their duty to be directly in charge of every manifestation of Catholic life, lest mistakes involving the Church be made and occasion for scandal be given. Not only the old outlook in general but also the unfortunate impression left on generations of priests by the lay-trustee troubles of an earlier time make it difficult to discard this attitude. But readiness to take the risks that go along with the encouragement of lay initiative—in the fields, for example, of education and communication—is called for by the present situation and by the mind of the Church. Unless these risks are taken there can only be sterility and, ultimately, death. Many new questions undoubtedly will arise. Catholic life may look quite different in another generation. But would we not rather have it look different than to see it fade into "innocuous desuetude"?

What is needed above all, perhaps by both clergy and laity, is the sense of belonging to a Church which by the will of God is involved in history, progressing toward the perfection willed for it by Christ—the perfection which He will give to it only at His return in glory. We need to gain the sense of Christ's presence precisely in such a Church, of the presence of the Holy Spirit to "lead you into all truth"—but not to guarantee its perfect expression in Catholic teaching or life in any generation. It is no criticism of the Church of past centuries to say that it was not perfect, that both its modes of thought and its practice can be improved upon, that it is repeatedly in need of renewal. The Church of the future will not be perfect either, but today we are called upon to run the risk of imperfection in a new way—to accept the hazards that go with freedom and activity rather than those that go with security and passivity.

Thus the very faithfulness of our clergy to the outlook in which they have been formed will make it possible for them to welcome the new outlook now that it is clearly the mind of the Church. For loyalty to the Church of Christ, so characteristic of the old outlook, will provide the motivation to adopt the new. However difficult the adjustment may prove to be, when *sentire cum Ecclesia* is seen to mean a change in accustomed ways of thought and action, loyalty will itself make the change possible. And, equally, now that loyalty to the Church is seen to demand pastoral work above all, priests will be happy to be freed from other burdens in order to carry out more effectively their essential priestly work as instruments of Christ, to bring God to men and men to God.

7

THE
INITIAL
EFFORT

THE CENTRAL aim of the renewal, as we have seen, is the formation of a Catholic people so open to the formation given by Christ and the Holy Spirit in the Church that they are continually enabled more fully to "practice the truth in love." In the Church of the future, then, all educational institutions, in the strict and in the more general sense of the term, will need to be ordered toward carrying out that aim.

Classes and courses and all the various media for the instruction of old and young will obviously need to be thought out afresh in this light. And so will the norms explicitly and implicitly proposed for family and parish life. Thus the Catholic family life of the future will have as its ideal not merely to pray together and stay together, but to help its members grow in the knowledge of Christ and send them out to carry on His work in the world, each according to his particular talent and vocation. The ideal parish life of the future will not merely provide parishioners with religious services and with activities that hold together a sociological group; it will be one which helps its members to "grow up in all things in Christ, the Head."

But if we are to evaluate our Catholic school system in terms of the renewal, we must keep in mind not only those specifications for the Church of the future but also the initial effort that will be required effectively to bring the renewal into American Catholic life—an unprecedented educational effort in every sense of the term.

Pope John XXIII, at the formal closing of the first session of the Council, indicated the dimensions of this effort as follows:

It will then be a question of extending to all departments of the life of the Church, social questions included, whatever the conciliar assembly may decide, and applying its norms to them with generous assent and prompt fulfillment. This most important phase will see bishops united in a gigantic effort of preaching sound doctrine and applying the law, which they themselves desire, and for this task will be called forth the collaboration of the forces of the diocesan and regular clergy, of the congregations of religious women, of the Catholic laity with all its attributes and potential, in order that the acts of the Fathers may be seconded by the most joyous and faithful response.

It will be a "new Pentecost" indeed, which will cause the Church to renew her interior riches and to extend her maternal care to every sphere of human activity. It will be a new advance of the Kingdom of Christ in the world, an elevated and persuasive reaffirmation of the good news of redemption, a clarion call of God's kingship, of the brotherhood of all men in charity, of the peace promised on earth to men of good will in accordance with God's good pleasure.

Obviously, if such a task is to be accomplished, it must take precedence for the time being over every other work—our bishops giving themselves wholly to it, marshaling all available resources, communicating enthusiasm and dedication, issuing practical directives and seeing that they are carried out.

What favorable factors can be counted upon? Above all, the fact that the renewal is grounded in the very nature of the Church and of the Christian message; for however startling the change in perspective may at first seem, it is more truly "natural" than the more legalistic and limited view of recent centuries. Likewise, the means of promoting the renewal already exist: in Holy Scripture, the liturgy, and the writings of the Fathers, as well as in modern scholarly works and in popular books and pamphlets—not to mention the living thought of all those who have shared in the various movements which have paved the way for the Council. Although an enormous work of synthesis and popularization remains to be done, the main lines of thought and endeavor have already been laid down.

Moreover, influenced by the various movements that have been preparing the way, many Catholics have been groping toward the traditional synthesis: some by way of social action, some by way of a new interest in Scripture, some through participation in the liturgy, some through a pastoral concern to form a living parish, still others by a search for the basic "spirituality" of the Church, or by the desire to lead a meaningful Christian lay life.

Further the pioneering work that has already been carried out here and there all tends to converge upon the same primary aims: to make worship meaningful and communal; to make the Bible available for public prayer and for personal nourishment; to involve parishioners not only in the material concerns of the parish but also in spreading the Good News and in ministering to the human needs of the community; to spread the knowledge of the Church's social teachings and to implement them by action. And all these attempts, scattered and fragmentary though they may have seemed, now provide a fund of practical experience upon which pastors, educators, and leaders may draw.

The great obstacle is, of course, inertia. But there can be no doubt that Catholics in this country have a very real loyalty to the Church and to the Pope. The fact that they are summoned by the Pope and their own bishops to make the great effort required for the renewal of Catholic life will in itself do much to arouse their enthusiasm.

Already the astonishingly widespread interest in the Council and in the spirit of ecumenism emanating from it are proving a powerful leaven. Along with non-Catholics, Catholics themselves are coming to realize that the Church is neither a static monolith nor a gigantic spiritual service station; they have begun to see it as a living organism, working in history, capable of change and development, responsive to the Spirit who breathes through it. Along with non-Catholics, they are coming to see that the truth the Church teaches is a living truth capable of being expressed in different ways, and that the life it communicates is a dynamic, fully human life, for here and now as well as hereafter. They have begun to feel that what happens in the Church can be really interesting, can really concern them—that the changes now in the wind may be expected to touch their own lives.

Certainly, no one expects that the work of renewal will be easy or that it will be accomplished overnight. It can be accomplished only by a total effort, one that demands careful planning, untiring persistence, and complete dedication.

Several dioceses both in the United States and Canada have already launched programs of their own for active participation in the Mass by holding three-day institutes, during which the clergy, the teachers of religion, and the laity of the diocese were shown in turn the bases and practical workings of participation; in addition, sermon outlines and other material were provided for pastors.

But it is now clear that much more will be required. The clergy will need the equivalent of a month's orientation period in order to make their own the new outlook in relation to Scripture, scriptural and liturgical theology, the liturgy, pastoral practice, ecumenism, and social action. The work of providing all priests with this orientation and freeing them to take advantage of it will, of course, add considerably, for a time, to the work of dioceses and religious houses. Yet it is obviously necessary if priests are to be able to give our bishops the intelligent and enthusiastic collaboration called for by the Pope.

In addition, the proposals made in the Constitution on the Liturgy will call for a reintegration of the entire program of studies in seminaries and for reorienting the whole formation of future priests along the same lines.

Similarly, what will be needed for Brothers and women religious is not merely a series of one-day sessions, or even lectures over a longer period of time, but a concerted effort on the part of superiors, retreatmasters, and directors to reorient the spiritual life of religious, in accordance with the genius of each order or congregation, along the lines of the renewal. Already the task is being undertaken by various new religious groups, and by some of the older congregations as well. Many already realize as well the urgent need to think out afresh the scope and function of their particular types of work in relation to today's requirements.

In the field of religious education, much more will obviously be required than new texts and courses, more even than the training of new teachers in the principles and methods of modern catechetics. Not only will all those who teach religion need to be formed in the new outlook, but also a greatly increased number of priests and religious will need to specialize in religious education in order to train new teachers and to provide retraining courses for all those already engaged in teaching.

Besides, more than such isolated programs as the one on participation in the Mass worked out by the

National Council of Catholic Men, or the one on community needs recommended by the National Council of Catholic Women will be required. Bishops, pastors, and directors will need to call upon all lay organizations—not as they have been called upon in the past, to direct their efforts to one or another good cause, but with a new urgency and to an effort of entirely new dimensions—to examine all their programs, to co-ordinate and integrate them so as most effectively to implement the renewal of all spheres of Catholic life.

Again, more than organizations will be needed. Something like the "Collegium" (that is, a group of "colleagues" studying together) established by Fr. Gremillion[1] will be required in parishes and dioceses —whether in the form of courses or informal groups —to involve both joiners and non-joiners in the effort to grasp the implications of the Council's program in personal and social life.

What will be required, in short, is a planned, multi-phased, co-ordinated effort to awaken Catholics to the possibilities of Christian living opened up by the new outlook, to help them realize those possibilities in communal worship, private prayer, organized activities, and in personal, social, and professional life. (One aspect of this effort should consequently be directed toward the elimination of religious junk— outstanding obstacles to the new outlook: the prayers, "art," "literature," and music which foster an unreal, sentimental kind of piety; the commercial-

[1] See J. C. Gremillion, *The Journal of a Southern Pastor* (Chicago: Fides Publishers, 1957); also *The Collegium Newsletter*, ed. by Msgr. Marvin Bordelon (Shreveport, Louisiana).

ism that promotes an equally commercialistic view of God's dealings with mankind; in short, everything that tends to sanction a magical, pietistic, or mechanistic view of the Christian religion.)

If our bishops were, singly and collectively, to devote themselves to implementing such a program, calling on priests, religious, and laity to make it effective, this would in itself do a great deal to clarify the purposes of the renewal. The fact that this kind of effort is now required, rather than a money-raising, bricks-and-mortar campaign, would help everyone to grasp the underlying purpose of the Church's organization and work—to "cast fire on the earth."

The laity would come to see that their role in the Church is not that of "keeping their purses open and their mouths shut," but that they too are called to take part in Christ's work for His Father and for mankind, giving to it all their intelligence, initiative, and skill. Priests, religious, and laity would realize afresh that we are all members of one another, living a life of ordered freedom under the leadership of the hierarchy, helping one another according to our different "ministries" to grow up in all things in Christ and to communicate His love to all men.

The foundations of this effort have already been laid down by a variety of movements in the Church —scriptural, theological, liturgical, and social—some of which, though in a partial and fragmentary way, have been influencing Catholic thinking and living for many decades. Now, modified and corrected where necessary, and integrated in a dynamic synthesis by the authoritative teaching voice of the Church, all

134

this work of the past is ready to be put at the service of the "new Pentecost" spoken of by the Pope.

If this "gigantic effort," as Pope John XXIII described it, is put into effect and gains momentum, we do not know what possibilities of Catholic living will unfold. If the effort is not made—if it is not begun even before the Council finishes it work—a unique opportunity will have been lost: the opportunity in our times to make the light and life of Christ in His Church seem truly relevant to the life of modern men.

Not that the new outlook, even were it to become the normal Catholic one, will suddenly transform us all into saints. Not that active participation in the liturgy, understood and carried out with a renewed sense of its meaning, will automatically fill us all with apostolic zeal. But ordinary Catholics will be able once more to think of themselves, not as servants who do not know what their Lord is doing, but as friends with whom He shares His life and work. They will be able to realize that they are called to grow in friendship with Him by meeting Him in the sacraments, in His Word, in His human brothers, and to cooperate with Him and give witness to His love by carrying out the work of human society "in the light of faith and with the dynamism of charity."

Of course, not every Catholic will respond equally to this new outlook; there will still be the half-hearted, the lukewarm, and the fall-aways (although it is quite possible that a kind of winnowing might take place, leaving the honest sinners but making a merely nominal practice of Catholicism quite out of the question). Nevertheless, as the outlook of the renewal begins to become the normal Catholic outlook, more and more Catholics will have a greater opportunity than at present to come into contact with Christ, with their minds and hearts as well as souls, and to realize the implications of their meeting Him in the "sacrament of the brother," to use H. A. von Balthasar's beautiful phrase.[2] And if we really believe that Christ is present and active in His Church, forming His people to His own likeness, that He is pouring out the Spirit on us in the sacraments, that He identifies Himself with each human person to be served and loved, we cannot but believe that such contact with Him will make a difference. Can we afford, then, not to make the effort, however unprecedented, that is required to communicate and implement the new outlook in the Church of America?

[2] H. A. von Balthasar, *Science, Religion and Christianity* (Westminster, Md.: Newman Press, 1958), pp. 142ff.

8

WITH OR
WITHOUT
A CATHOLIC
SCHOOL
SYSTEM

CATHOLIC schools and colleges must, of course, be taken very seriously into account in the work of inaugurating the renewal sketched out in the previous chapter. Our educational system is very much with us; it is an important factor in forming those whom it reaches—the more so since what is taught and inculcated in Catholic schools and colleges is so largely taken as the norm of what should be given to all young people. One aspect of the "gigantic effort" spoken of by Pope John XXIII must certainly be the communication of the new outlook to all teachers and administrators in Catholic educational institutions. And certainly this large body of dedicated men and women will be among the most eager to follow the Council's directives in their personal spirituality and in their professional work.

But in planning for the future another question arises: Can we afford, when the need for the religious formation of the whole Catholic people is so great, to provide a general education for all or even a part of our young people?

Obviously a great increase in directly pastoral work will be required to implement the new outlook. Parish priests will need to devote much thought and effort to the celebration of the rites of the Church in such a way as to involve the faithful, and to the preparation of sermons which will really open out to their people the relevance of the scriptural passages and of the sacramental rites. Not only the Sunday Mass, but also baptisms, weddings, wakes, funerals, and parish devotions will need to be conducted so that they may become occasions of real growth in the knowledge of Christ for everyone who takes part in them.

Not less important will be the pastoral work of "coaching" the members of the parish in the Christian life, not only by sermons and other forms of group instruction but by the direct personal contact which alone can uncover the various material, psychophysical, intellectual, and spiritual obstacles which keep so many people from meeting with Christ in the Church. This work has already been defined as the most important task of the pastor in present-day parish life;[1] its importance shines out even more clearly in the light of the new outlook. Removing many of these obstacles will in turn mean enlisting the aid of

---

[1] See C. S. Nuesse and Thomas H. Harte, eds., *The Sociology of the Parish: An Introductory Symposium* (Milwaukee: Bruce Publishing Company, 1951). Joseph H. Fichter in "Church Attendance," *America,* June 8, 1963, reports on a nation-wide study of young men aged 18-22 that good clergy-lay relations emerged as the most important factor in continued church attendance at this age.

lay individuals and agencies—an undertaking which calls for both time and strength. A further demand upon the energy of parish priests will be made by the ecumenical aspects of the renewal—fostering communication with the other churches in their neighborhoods, and concerning themselves with the needs and problems of the whole community.

In view of all these demands, it is certainly to be hoped that one effect of the Council will be a simpler and more integrated prayer life for priests; as things are, to carry out the various un-co-ordinated spiritual exercises which are either commanded or strongly urged would take at least three or four hours a day. Another desideratum is the elimination of much of the administrative red tape, particularly that connected with marriages, which now takes so much of a parish priest's time. A third is to provide pastors with more assistance, not only from lay people but also perhaps from permanent deacons.

In any event, this program of pastoral work will require a maximum of the priest's time and attention; it would seem also to call for numerous small or middle-sized parishes in place of the vast ones still so common in some urban areas. How much pastoral energy, then, will the Church of the future be able to spare for the work of building, maintaining, and administering schools? How many priests will it be able to spare for the work of general, as opposed to religious, education?

Again, the new outlook will require greatly increased attention to all the aspects of religious formation, on the part not of priests alone but of all those who in any way assist in the work of the teaching

Church. Many experts in catechetics will be needed to train all those who teach religion, to advise parents, to help plan and carry out programs utilizing religious and mass media to the best advantage. New ways and means will be needed to reach persons and groups with special needs and those outside the regular parish framework, so that all the faithful will be given the opportunity in some way to be drawn into the vivifying current of the renewal.

And finally, not only parish priests but also parishioners will need to give new thought, time, and effort to increasing communication between themselves and other religious groups, and to taking part in the concerns of the general community.

Will the Church of the future be able to fulfill all these demands and at the same time maintain a system of general education? After all, the state today provides a basic education for all its citizens. Is it reasonable to expect the Church to continue also to offer the same service at the expense of those services which it alone can provide?

In the immediate past, as we have seen, it seemed almost impossible to carry out the task of the Catholic formation of children and young people apart from Catholic schools; and certainly that task must be carried out if the renewal is to continue in the generations to come.

If Catholic schools are really necessary for salvation, obviously we must continue to provide them—as many as possible, at whatever cost. But now we need to ask ourselves: Will a Catholic school system be needed in the future?

In the past, the question of providing religious formation for the young outside of Catholic schools has been seen primarily in terms of finding adequate teachers and providing suitable times and places. These are, certainly, real and practical problems. But the new outlook places them in a different perspective. As the focus of formation shifts from the classroom to the church and to daily life, the work of formation must become more that of the pastor, the parent, the "coach" in the Christian life, than that of the teacher. Formation so conceived is not primarily the task of the schools. May it not be possible, then, that it could be adequately provided outside the schools?

In the past, practically the whole burden of the formation and instruction of Catholic children not enrolled in Catholic schools was laid on the weekly catechism class. The new outlook, however, envisions formal religious instruction as ancillary to the formation and instruction given by Christ Himself, above all in the Sunday Mass. Children quite naturally "learn by doing." The weekly experience of taking part with a *praying community* in hearing and responding to God's message, in offering the sacrifice and receiving Communion, is capable of forming their minds and hearts as mere attendance at Mass with others merely attending Mass does not. Moreover, they will realize that the scriptural readings, the sermon, the sacramental signs, are meant to be understood and that this understanding is something for them to grow into—an attitude that is all important.

Again, when Sunday Mass truly becomes the focus of Catholic life and when parish devotions and activities also have been oriented toward "hearing the Word of God and putting it into practice," parents will be in a better position to instruct their own children in Christian living. As parents come to realize that taking part in Sunday Mass is the supreme privilege of the Christian life and not a mere obligation to be fulfilled, their attitude will communicate itself to their children.

The majority of Catholic parents today are terrified at the thought of instructing their children in Christian truth because they assume that one must be an expert theologian to do it properly. As they come to realize that the work of instruction which they are called on to perform is primarily that of familiarization with a Person—with His personality, His work, His dealings with human beings—then they will see it as something at least potentially within their competence and something that can be carried out mainly in the normal course of family life.

In the same way, as parents become aware of the spirit and aims of the renewal, their efforts to train their children in Christian prayer will be a matter not of making sure that they know set forms of prayer, but rather of opening out to each child the possibility of personal conversation with His Father in heaven and with Christ his Brother. And discipline will be less a matter of inculcating unthinking obedience than of arousing the children's sense of personal responsibility for responding to God's love.

Even under present conditions, it has been found quite feasible to call upon parents to prepare their own children for First Confession and First Communion. In at least one parish, where the majority of the people are not particularly well educated but where the climate of participation has been cultivated for some years, the parents of First Communion candidates are now given some instruction and suitable texts; they then prepare their own children and, naturally, learn a great deal themselves in doing so.

Of course, there will always be parents who take little or no responsibility for the religious formation of their children; for such cases special provision will have to be made. But parents are generally eager and grateful for advice and help; they are certainly more concerned with their children's religious formation than with their own. Once they are shown that the former requires the latter, they will have this special and strong incentive to cooperate with the whole process of the renewal.

The main problem, then, will be to show parents what the task of religious formation really entails, and to help them work out its practical application in family life. On the parish level special "workshops" for parents are needed to discuss ways in which parents can familiarize their children with Christ and so with the Father, and with the great plan of salvation that centers in Christ, the plan unfolded in scripture, the liturgy, and Catholic doctrine, the plan in which we participate through worship and Christian living.

In the modern situation, certainly, more is needed. We cannot expect the formation of young people to be left, as it was in early Christian times, entirely to the liturgy and the home. The home is no longer the center it once was; as the children grow older, there is always the opportunity for formation but less and

143

less for even informal instruction. And besides, children need to receive God's truth and to receive guidance in the Christian life from personalities other than their parents, if only to help them distinguish between their feelings toward their parents and their feelings toward their Father in heaven.

However, with community participation in the Mass in the full sense of the renewal, it may well be that a lesser amount of formal religious instruction will seem desirable. A weekly class and a two-week vacation school are admittedly inadequate in the present situation. But in the climate of the renewal, the task of formal religious instruction would be simply to round out and give the beginnings of systematic apprehension to the religious knowledge gathered in church and home. The once-a-week-class and vacation school setup may, then, on the grade school level, prove quite adequate to the new situation.

But a rather different program would seem to be desirable on the high-school level. Young people at this age need above all to discover the relevance of their Christian relation with God to the new aspects of life being opened out to them—the relevance of Christian truth to the general knowledge they are acquiring and, still more, to the questions they are beginning to ask of life. They do not so much need information about religion as they need personal guidance toward a truly religious view of life in all its aspects, a guidance that can help to remove obstacles to a real and enthusiastic commitment to Christ.

What would therefore be desirable, in the climate and framework of the renewal, would seem to be a guidance program, provided by the diocese or parish and perhaps given in conjunction with the public-school guidance program, in which experienced counselors could help each adolescent to find himself, in relation to God and his fellow men. The process of clearing away the emotional and intellectual obstacles to his doing so could be furthered by group counseling, carried out perhaps in a released-time setup, in which, under expert guidance, young Catholics could discuss problems of religious living and thus help one another in solving them. In the course of this group counseling the young people could also be guided toward an outward-looking view of their community and its needs and toward filling some of these needs— providing help for understaffed hospitals, for example (as teen-agers already do in some communities), reading to blind persons, and so on. Again, those with a special interest in some aspect of Christian truth could be provided with further guidance and with reading material to fit their needs.

As for religious formation outside of school, we have the example of the Jewish groups which, although not generally concerned with setting up full-time schools of their own, have provided their young people with "Hebrew schools." That children can be formed, religiously and culturally, outside of school hours there can be no question; these Jewish groups have succeeded in doing so.

In today's atmosphere, we might well gain increased assistance from both Jewish and Protestant groups. Members of many other faiths besides our own are increasingly concerned with problems of religious formation. We could unite with them in a common effort to make out-of-school religious instruction a normal part of community life, just as in many places "Bible schools" and "vacation schools" are accepted as part of the summer's schedule for children of various faiths. Or, again, if shared time is a possibility, so is the idea of more adequate released time. A plan intended to make this arrangement more viable by grouping schools of religion for the various faiths near the public school, thus eliminating problems of transportation and easing those of scheduling, has already been proposed.[2]

How is such instruction for children and young people to be provided? The Confraternity of Christian Doctrine is the canonically established organization, presumably set up in every parish, for precisely this purpose of religious instruction. Its complete program, to be carried out under the supervision of a parish board, provides training for teachers, special aids for parents, weekly classes and vacation schools for grade-school children, classes or discussion circles for adolescents and adults, and public-relations work.

As has frequently been pointed out, in most parishes the Confraternity so far has been operating under enormous difficulties. It has too often been considered only a makeshift until parochial schools could accommodate all Catholic children. In many parishes it has never been taken seriously; its work has been reduced to that of providing classes at the grade-school level—too often, even at best, taught by Sisters exhausted after a week's school teaching, or by willing but inadequately trained lay teachers, and at worst

[2] James E. McClellan, "Needed: A New Philosophy of Parochial Education," *Christianity and Crisis*, XVII: 9.

by completely untrained high-school boys and girls. More and more authorities are coming to realize that in today's situation the work of the Confraternity is essential and must be given its due place in diocesan and parish planning. Dioceses are making new attempts to bring home to pastors and people the importance and scope of its task. New training courses for teachers are being offered, and new attempts are being made to enlist suitable candidates.

In the context of the renewal, all this effort could become more fruitful. The work of the Confraternity would be oriented toward parish worship and would find there its proper completion. It would not any longer seem, as it so often does now, something foreign to other parish concerns, for which the pastor alone is responsible, and which is to be handled simply by engaging Sisters from the nearest Catholic school to teach the younger children. Rather, it would become an essential part of parish life, a concern which the whole Catholic community would share with their pastor.

Where more appeared to be needed, the establishment of a parish school of religion might be indicated. Such a school, at Fairport, New York, was described at length in *America* for January 21, 1961:

Four years ago Father Kelly built the Assumption School of Religion on a property adjacent to a new large public school. With an investment of only $150,000 and four nuns, Father Kelly, who has no other parochial school, handles the religious instruction of 700 Catholic students—550 elementary and 150 high school. Each child comes one full hour per week on a staggered released-time program which operates during all the hours of the school day. The First Communion and Confirmation classes come an additional hour after school. In modern classrooms with up-to-date books and visual aids, each teacher handles about 25 students at a time. There are 40 religion classes a week. . . . Our children—all of them—come to religion class with enthusiasm. It is the high point of the week in their school world. In addition, the children attend Mass regularly and receive the sacraments frequently. . . . The Sisters also have time for other parish work. They visit lax Catholics, maintain an accurate parish census, and promote the full program of the Confraternity of Christian Doctrine. Within three years, our Sisters (Mission Helpers of the Sacred Heart) trained 150 adults as lay catechists for our own and twenty other parishes. This religion school has an enviable record, almost 100 per cent attendance of all public school children, and this attendance is enthusiastic.

All of this suggests that in the climate of the renewal the problem of the Christian formation of young people, which at present seems to be insoluble outside of Catholic schools, could be resolved in the context of the formation of the whole Catholic community of worship, of growth in the knowledge of God, of active charity and neighborliness toward all the other members of the human community.

Experts say that the same thing is true of the problem of providing religious formation for Catholic students in secular colleges and universities. The question is not one of "saving the faith" of these students but of "incarnating the Church" on these campuses, to use the phrase of Monsignor Alexander Sigur, National Chaplain of the Newman Apostolate, whose recent article in *America* sums up Newman Club thinking and experience as to what could be done and needs to be done:

The Newman Apostolate can establish true schools of theology, with qualified faculty and administration, introducing religion as intellectually respectable and offering courses for academic credit in the main stream of higher education. Religious orders can prepare men and women for teaching positions within American secular colleges and universities, where the riches in Catholic culture and insight can become part of the great conversation. Architecturally excellent and liturgically fitting centers of worship will offer a pivot for Catholics present on any campus community. Our Newman facilities must be the center of Catholic culture on the campus. Chairs of theology and Catholic studies (like Harvard's Stillman professorship), and programs in Christian culture and Church history should be endowed at outstanding institutions, where serious and lasting entry can be made into the world of learning. Bishops and superiors of religious orders might continue to make generous provision of manpower and facilities for the group of key Catholic leaders in the secular campus community. Catholic lay professors, steeped in the Christian humanistic tradition, will work side by side with their truth-questing colleagues and share a mutual concern and common discovery. Cognate—if not identical—Christian goals inspire many of our associates in the learning and teaching community. We can pursue these goals together in an environment which, above all others, should provide a healthy atmosphere for ecumenical endeavor.[3]

Monsignor Sigur's proposals clearly are in harmony with the aims and the spirit of the new outlook. If these proposals were implemented, the formation of Catholic students on secular campuses would be taken care of as, with rare exceptions, it is not under present circumstances, and other goals be achieved as well.

It would seem, then, that in the context of the renewal, the problem of the Christian formation of young Catholics outside Catholic schools and colleges could be solved. It has not been solved hitherto. But, clearly, it must be unless we can provide Catholic schooling for all Catholic young people. Would it not, then, be more realistic to devote our resources to implementing this solution for the benefit of all our young people and the whole Catholic community, rather than continue to provide a complete Catholic education for a part of our young people only?

In the past, we have considered the Catholic school and college to be the central means—and the normal one—of providing religious formation. We have not seriously tried to think out any other approach. The new outlook clearly implies that the school will no longer be central; its function now appears as ancillary. If we were to begin thinking of the church-

[3] "Newman Raises Its Sights," *America,* September 1, 1962. See also John A. O'Brien, "Catholic Students in Secular Colleges," *St. Jude,* May and June, 1961; George A. Fitzgerald, "Catholics in Secular Colleges," *America,* May 21, 1960.

home-additional aids pattern as the normal one through the high-school years, and the "incarnation of the Church on secular campuses" as the normal objective on the higher levels, would we not be working along lines potentially far more fruitful than those followed at present?

The great reason for establishing our Catholic school system in the first place, and the reason many people will certainly bring up to justify its continued existence today, is the fear that a widespread loss of faith would result if Catholics attended the public schools. Even under present conditions, there would seem to be little real basis for this fear. Surveys indicate that the regularity of Catholic practice is only slightly higher among adults who have attended Catholic schools and colleges than among those who have not.[4] Catholic schooling does not seem to make the great difference that might have been expected. It should also be considered that, before the present crisis of numbers, those who took the trouble to help build and maintain a Catholic school, or who moved near one so that their children might have the benefit of a Catholic education, were the more zealous Catholic parents. The slight edge held by the Catholic-

[4] Peter A. Rossi and Andrew M. Greeley, "The Impact of the Roman Catholic Denominational School," *The School Review*, Spring, 1964. See also Peter and Alice Rossi, "Some Effects of Parochial School Education in America," *Daedalus*, Spring, 1961, pp. 300-328. These authors are at present engaged on a major study, financed by the Carnegie Corporation, of the effects of Catholic education. The data previously available have been admittedly fragmentary. Joseph Fichter (*art. cit.*) lists Catholic schooling as of importance in continued church attendance only after contacts with priests and the religious practices of the parents.

schooled over other Catholics with regard to religious practice may thus very well be due as much to the home as to the school. Therefore, if a serious effort were made to provide adequate liturgical and home formation, coupled with formal religious instruction, for all Catholics, in place of the attempt to maintain our present educational system, it is hard to see why there need be any fear of a decline in membership. The proportion of practicing Catholics might, on the contrary, be expected to improve.

If we were thus to make outside-of-school formation and instruction the norm for young Catholics, the Catholic school would cease to be the presumed rule and become the recognized exception. There will no doubt always be Catholic parents who want a type of education for their children other than that given in the public schools and who both can and will support it. Again, there will always be boys and girls who could benefit from a boarding-school education, especially on the secondary level, and parents whose circumstances make such schools possible or desirable. Catholic schools would have a genuine function here, since these young people, separated from parish and home influences, might otherwise receive no Catholic formation. In the educational scheme of the country these schools would have the same place and function as other private schools; they would in no way parallel or compete with the function of the public schools, nor would they constitute a system involving the diocese or the parish in the work of general education.

In some city areas, it is true, there might conceivably be a need for schools supported by the diocese for the benefit of children whose parents were clearly incapable of giving them adequate home formation. Similar schools for the chlidren of large groups of new immigrants might serve them as the parochial schools served immigrant groups in the past. But these schools might be the responsibility of the diocese rather than the parish; and they would hardly be so numerous or so uniform as to require a school system.

It can be agreed that some Catholic schools will be needed. The question is whether, in view of the aims of the renewal, the Catholic school system as a whole will any longer be necessary. The same question may be asked concerning our colleges. If the effort to "incarnate the Church on secular campuses" were to replace the present effort to maintain *all* our two hundred eighty-two colleges and universities, should we not have much to gain?

More and more Catholics would be reached as Catholic centers on secular campuses were enlarged and multiplied. There would be immensely increased opportunities for the cross-fertilization of Catholic thought with Protestant, Jewish, and secular thinking—opportunities to carry on what Monsignor Sigur calls "the great conversation." Catholics educated in such an atmosphere would be all the better prepared to be Catholic members of their own local communities and of the intellectual community at large.[5]

At the present time there are many more Catholics

---

[5] As to the fear that Catholics will lose their faith on non-Catholic campuses, authorities agree that the rare cases of loss of faith are due rather to previous indifference, poor home influences, and inadequate preparation rather than to the influence of the college or university (*art. cit.,* note 3).

on secular than on Catholic campuses, and everything seems to indicate that the proportion in secular institutions will be much greater as time goes on. The numbers of young people going to college are expected to increase enormously, but of these numbers the private colleges will be handling a smaller and smaller proportion. Unless substantial federal aid is given to private colleges, those not heavily endowed will have to price themselves out of reach of all but the wealthy.

Under the circumstances, might not the wise course of action be to cease resisting these trends, to give up the effort to maintain a large number of Catholic institutions of higher learning and establish still others? Efforts at this level might far more fruitfully be devoted to carrying out on secular campuses the Newman programs outlined by Monsignor Sigur, and to maintaining and strengthening those Catholic institutions which seemed capable of making some significant contribution to the intellectual life of the Church and of our country. One other possibility would be the establishment of Catholic colleges within secular universities; St. Michael's at the University of Toronto is an example. More and more Catholics are, in actual fact, going to be on secular campuses. Would it not be better, then, to accept this as the normal situation, and to plan and work accordingly?

But, some Catholics will say, granted that better provision needs to be made for the formation of Catholic young people of all ages outside of our Catholic school and college setup; is there no possibility of doing so and at the same time of maintaining, perhaps even expanding, our Catholic school system? With a more adequate church and home formation and with an educational system permeated with the spirit of the renewal, what wonderful Catholics might be graduated from our schools and colleges!

One further question needs to be asked: Given the climate of the renewal, would children educated in a Catholic school system in fact be better formed for Christian life in today's world than children who had attended public schools? Even supposing we could continue to maintain our Catholic school system and at the same time provide adequate religious formation for the whole Catholic body, would it be desirable to do so?

We may suppose, for the sake of argument, that the religious formation given in the Catholic school system of the future would be so reoriented as to further the aims of the renewal—and, as should be obvious from earlier chapters, this would indeed require a revolution. Religion class would no longer be just another subject, but something quite distinct from the regular school routine. Teachers of religion, all thoroughly trained in the spirit and methods of the new catechetics, would foster not only interest but a genuine spirit of inquiry. The school's prayer life would be patterned after that of the Church, integrated with the Church's feasts and seasons, and steeped in Holy Scripture. School discipline would not bear on religious practice, school authority would not clothe itself in the authority of the Church, so that no child would be led to carry over resentment against school authority into resentment against the authority of the Church; his relation with Christ, his free commitment to Christ, would be fostered and not jeopardized. The school would, moreover, do everything possible to encourage friendliness and respect toward the public school and those who attend it.

But even if all this could be put into effect in the Catholic school system, it does not seem likely that an integrally Catholic education would result. It would be a case, rather, of new wine in old wineskins, for the old religious outlook harmonizes well enough with the present general ethos of public education; the new outlook would be at odds with it. An integrally Catholic education would be truly humanistic, in the sense that it would foster, above all, the development of each student's human powers and train him in the skills necessary for full human living; it would not mainly load him with facts and drill him in processes, as American education too generally does today. Such an education, again, would foster a sense of responsibility for self-development for the sake of serving one's fellow men, rather than, as at present, encouraging students to think of diplomas as magic passports to security and success. But until a revolution in the philosophy of public education itself has occurred in this country, it is hard to believe that the Catholic school system itself could be transformed along these lines and carry them even further so as to give a humanistic *Christian* formation. In the private Catholic school the possibility does exist. But for any large school system the pressures toward conformity are simply too great—the pressures exerted by standards, teacher-training agen-

156

cies, texts, and the whole elaborate paraphernalia of present-day instruction. It is true that some hopeful trends are beginning to be discernible—for example, in the "new arithmetic," in various experiments with reading methods, and in allowing students to go ahead at their own pace. But it would seem as though Catholic educators and the Catholic public as a whole could work much more effectively to promote these tendencies from within the public school system than by trying to reform their own system separately. In the meantime, it would seem more fruitful to try to give Catholic young people, in the course of their outside-of-school formation, a truly humanistic and Christian motivation for pursuing their education than to try to do so within the framework of a Catholic education in which the greater part of the courses and teaching methods were differently oriented.

But this is not all. Even if it were possible to reform Catholic education completely, I am not convinced that attendance at a Catholic school would be the best way of preparing a young person for Catholic living in today's world. The atmosphere of a Catholic school is by nature a sheltered, even a hothouse one. True, outside of school the child or young person may have friends who are not Catholics. But most of his day is spent in Catholic surroundings; he does not become accustomed to the massive impact of the prevailingly secular atmosphere in which he will ordinarily be required to live his adult life. He is not prepared to stand up against the cold wind of indifference; he is more likely to be reacting against what seems like the over-religiousness of the Catholic school.

A Catholic education may perhaps fit a young person intellectually for some kind of dialogue with those of other faiths or of no faith at all. He may be taught the doctrines of the Catholic Church, and something about the doctrines that Protestant bodies hold in common with his own; he may learn to value the Judaic aspect of the Christian heritage. He may be equipped with reasonable bases for belief in God designed to meet the arguments of unbelievers. But except as his associations outside of school bring him into actual contact with different points of view, all this remains abstract. Learning his faith in school, learning general subjects in a Catholic atmosphere, he easily comes to feel either that religion is properly confined within the circle of one's coreligionists, or else that he knows all the answers—and neither of these attitudes is that of true dialogue.

It has already been remarked that by bringing about the association of Catholic parents with each other rather than with those of other faiths, by identifying their community interests with those of the parochial school, that school cannot help working against ecumenism in still another way.

It seems doubtful, consequently, whether the Catholic school system, however completely renewed, could compensate for the very fact of being a system. What half a century ago still seemed to be its great advantages—getting the children together in a Catholic atmosphere and keeping them apart from non-Catholics—now appear to be serious disadvantages. This is true whether we envisage our educational system as extending from the kindergarten through the Ph.D. or as being limited to some particular level.

If a young person receives his whole education under Catholic auspices, he suffers the disadvantages of a hothouse atmosphere almost from the cradle to maturity. If we limit our efforts to maintaining our grade schools, as was mainly done in the past, we shall be training the children in this hothouse atmosphere and then leaving them, just at adolescence, to adjust to the atmosphere of a secular society as well as to their own new situation.

If we were, instead, to follow what has been the more recent trend and concentrate on high schools, we should be putting young persons into a segregated Catholic situation just when they need to begin to realize the impact of secularism and to learn how to resist it, just when they begin to become aware of other personalities and need to learn how to meet them in charity while differing from them on one or another conviction.

What if we were to drop the grade and high school systems entirely, and concentrate on colleges? Clearly, the result would be to cut young Catholics off from the intellectual currents of the general academic community just when they need to discover the relevance of Catholic truth to these currents and the reality of Catholic life in a secular world.

Neither, in the light of the renewal, does shared time seem to offer a truly satisfactory formation. Its effect on the students, as in our present school system, would be to make of religion simply another subject, taught in the same atmosphere and seemingly on the same level as history, literature, and the social sciences. It would also lend support to the notion that religion influences one's views of literature and the social sciences but not those concerning science or athletics, as well as to the assumption, already implicit in too much of today's student thinking, that what is taught in science classes is incontrovertibly true whereas what is taught in religion and the humanities is a matter of opinion.

Moreover, this plan would segregate Catholics, teachers and students alike, both from other believers and from nonbelievers in areas where the direct impact of other points of view is most crucial. Worse still, it would suggest that there must necessarily be a Catholic, a Protestant, and a Jewish version of each of the social sciences, instead of encouraging those of all faiths to work toward a truly ecumenical interchange. In spite of its apparent advantages, then, shared time may prove to be a kind of educational will-o'-the-wisp, with a tendency to distract concerned persons of all faiths from the basic problems of religious formation in our own day.

In the context of the new outlook, two major conclusions would seem to be inevitable: first, that a truly Catholic formation for all young people is a real possibility if we use all the resources at our disposal; and second, that a general education under Catholic auspices is no longer as necessary or even as desirable as in the past. As things are, the maintenance of our Catholic school system—not to speak of its extension—takes up a large part of our available human resources, resources now needed for urgent *religious* tasks. Even if some form of public aid were to relieve us of part of the financial burden, should we, then, plan for the continued maintenance of our Catholic school system in the future?

9

NEW
RESOURCES
FOR THE
CHURCH

IF WE begin to consider the resources which would become available to the American Church—for its own needs, for those of the Church in South America, and for those of the world—if our educational system were suddenly to be disestablished, the prospects are quite startling.

Think of the time that a bishop would have at his disposal: time now spent in attending commencements, laying cornerstones, opening new buildings, and giving awards for spelling bees, in attending long meetings concerned with real estate and construction, in negotiating for the Brothers and Sisters needed to staff new schools, and so on and on.

Think of the time that a pastor would have to devote to the needs of his flock: time now spent in giving out report cards, in attending school contests, band concerts, and other school events, in meetings to arrange for raffles, fairs, and bingo parties, in wrestling with the myriad details of maintenance and administration.

Think of the nearly 13,000 priests who would be

freed for other work: for pastoral care in the diocese, for work with newly arrived immigrants, migrant workers, divorced Catholics, and young working people. Think of the nearly 4,000 priests now teaching on the college level, many of them already equipped for extending and deepening the work of the Newman Clubs. Think of South America, where the need for priests is so urgent if the faith there is to survive at all.

Think of the more than 5,000 Brothers who would be available to work with special groups, such as school dropouts, delinquents, and pre-delinquents, to help with counseling programs, Newman Club work, and countless other projects.

Think of the more than 103,000 Sisters who would likewise be freed to help with Newman Club work, with parish programs of instruction, and with other greatly needed projects such as residences for young working girls and for the aging, home care of the sick. One can only begin to imagine the many vital and needed services, now hardly touched, which women religious could perform in our own country, quite aside from the call of South America and of other mission fields.

Think, too, of the witness given by the Church in our world, if such numbers of religious were to be brought out of schools and colleges into ordinary parish life, where their light could shine "to all who are in the house" and not merely to their own students; if diocesan priests had enough time for pastoral work so that they could be genuinely in touch with all the members of their flock; if enough priests and religious worked on secular campuses so that they could come to be known by great numbers of young people, Catholic and non-Catholic; if priests and religious were meeting the needs of problem groups not as yet cared for by society! All this might also result in a great increase of vocations. As things are, innumerable Catholic young people never have a real opportunity to meet a priest; many never have the opportunity to become really acquainted with religious and their work, and thus do not even consider the possibility of a priestly or religious vocation.

Think of the 17,000 lay teachers now in Catholic colleges who might find their place in an expanding program of public higher education, sharing in and contributing to the intellectual life of these communities. Think of the nearly 13,000 lay teachers on the secondary level, the more than 32,000 on the elementary level, who would reinforce the efforts of their colleagues already teaching and administering in the public schools toward building up a truly humanistic public education.

Think of the tremendous amount of lay effort now devoted to the material needs of Catholic schools and colleges which would be freed for wider interests. Redirected away from a narrow concern with the parish school and its financial requirements, parents would be in a position both to devote their attention to the Church and to act more fully as responsible members of the community as a whole. And parish life itself, no longer so centered around the school and those concerned with the school, could more easily reach out to include all the members of the parish in its life and work.

Think, too, of the buildings which might now become parish centers or schools of religion, or serve some other community purpose.

Think, finally, of the $100,000,000 (the 1960 figure) spent annually on parochial-school maintenance, operation, and renovation, and of the vast sums used for the same purposes by Catholic high schools and colleges. Think of the tens of millions of dollars (the figure in 1958 was $157 million) now going each year for new construction, which would then be available instead for parish programs of religious instruction, for Newman Club work, for urgently needed services to special groups, and for all the other works of the Church in this country—as well as for missions in every other part of the world.

Of course, nothing like this could happen all at once. The disestablishment of the Catholic educational system would necessarily mean arranging for the gradual absorption into the public school system, at a different tempo in each community, of the children and young people now cared for in Catholic schools. It would mean training young religious for new types of work—not suddenly sending those who have been teaching general subjects for many years out into different fields. It would mean initiating the means and methods for providing a religious formation for all Catholics before the Catholic school system ceased to exist. Above all, it would require that the work of the renewal be already begun, and that clergy, religious, and laity alike be agreed, in the light of the new outlook, that the Catholic educational system to which so much heroic effort had been devoted had now served its purpose—that the needs of the Church now lie elsewhere.

The transition would obviously not be easy. But even as it was made, it would itself provide the resources needed to carry on and complete the renewal called for by the Council here in our own country and all over the world. And how incalculably great a tragedy it would be if, instead, we allowed our educational system gradually to be "contained," to become static, and to reach a smaller and smaller proportion of our young people—while still consuming so much of the manpower, effort, and material resources of the Church—while we take no adequate measures to provide religious formation for all the others. This, certainly, is the great danger inherent in the present situation.

10

A NEW CLIMATE IN THE CHURCH

SOME readers of this book may still be unconvinced that the major task facing the Church today is to communicate to all its members what we have been calling "the new outlook" and to implement it in all aspects of Catholic life. They may feel that such a program is all very well for an elite, but that any attempt to carry it out on the scale outlined in the preceding chapters would only serve to distract the Church from the work of saving men's souls by seeing to it that they assent to Catholic beliefs, that they obey the Ten Commandments of God and the seven commandments of the Church, and that they carry out at least the minimum of religious practice enjoined by those commandments. From this point of view, the Catholic school system is a time-tested means of achieving these objectives. How can anyone suggest that it be abandoned?

To such readers I can only repeat that theirs might be a valid point of view if we were still in the climate of the last few hundred years—the climate of a

Church intent on self-preservation, spending its efforts to hold its own, to preserve, to fight off attacks, to centralize authority, and to maintain order within the ranks. In such a climate it does not seem to matter very much what a few enthusiasts may do to promote a more meaningful worship or a more authentic Catholic witness in the world, so long as these efforts do not interfere with the Church's essentially protective role toward both her institutions and her members. But, since the calling of the Second Vatican Council, a new climate has been created.

The new climate, first of all, calls for a new diffusion of responsibility. When the bishops of the Church assembled in solemn council, they found that they had not been called together to rubber-stamp a set of conclusions already arrived at but to act as the successors of the Apostles: as a body responsible, under the leadership but not the domination of the Holy Father, for the well-being of the Church. This episcopal responsibility—not simply for the orderly administration of a diocese but rather for the very life of the Church—will almost certainly be codified and perpetuated in conciliar decrees as to the nature and function of the episcopacy, and also by the establishment of national episcopal bodies as regularly functioning parts of the organism of the Church.

The same principle of subsidiarity may then be expected to be extended throughout the Church; in particular, the responsibilities of the layman with regard both to the Church and to his own work in the world are expected to be clarified. The spirit of the past was one of limiting and centralizing responsibility, with the layman responsible only for his own belief and obedience. The spirit of the renewal calls every Catholic to share, according to his place and function in the Church, in responsibility for its growth and welfare and for the communication of the life and charity of Christ to all men.

The new climate is, again, characterized by a search for unity without the desire to impose uniformity. In approving the introduction and first part of the Constitution on the Liturgy, the assembled Council Fathers agreed in principle that the bishops of each country are to be responsible for adapting certain aspects of the liturgy to the needs of their people— thus breaking up the uniformity imposed on the Roman rite some four hundred years ago. No longer is it possible to decry as heretical the idea that modern languages might be far more widely used in the liturgy of the Roman rite, since the Council Fathers explicitly approved of this form of adaptation. Uniformity in the language of worship thus gives way to the possibility of greater unity of hearts and minds brought about by a closer, more intelligent encounter with Christ in worship and public prayer.

Again, the explicit enunciation by the Holy Father that Christian truth may be expressed in different ways, to suit the needs of different mentalities, opens the way to a search for the ways in which Christ's unchanging message and life may best be expressed in the various idioms of different cultures and levels of cultivation. In such a development, the living apprehension of Christ's truth is all-important for every Catholic; the mere memorizing of one or another formulation of it can no longer seem a valid goal of religious instruction.

The new climate is, therefore, one of openness: we

are no longer, in fear or distrust or indifference, to shut ourselves off from our non-Catholic neighbors, but to look for what we have in common even while recognizing no less clearly where we differ. We are to work with them in pursuit of common goals; to make the concerns of all men our own.

And so the new climate is one of freedom. It is now clear that an unthinking conformity to commands imposed from without, a merely habitual regularity with regard to religious practice, a mere notional assent to doctrines, are not what the times require of Catholics in any walk of life; they are in fact incompatible with the Christian life. Pope John XXIII, in his encyclical *Pacem in Terris,* wrote that every man has the right "to worship God according to the dictates of an upright conscience"; and this surely means that Catholics, too, must worship God from inner conviction, not under the compulsion of habit. It means that each human person is responsible for accepting or rejecting the freedom that Christ came to bring; that the teaching Church, the hierarchy and clergy, cannot save the souls of the Church's members without their own free, personal, and authentic acceptance of the Gospel's message, their own freely given response to it. Certainly, God works in us "both the willing and the doing," but He does so in such a way that these are our free acts—acts nobody else can perform for us.

The task of the teaching Church and of all who share in its work is, therefore, to bring persons to Christ living and present in the Church, to proclaim and open out His message, to remove obstacles to men's meeting with Him—never to make assent to formulas a substitute for true consent to Christian truth, or routine habit for fully human activity, or compulsion of any kind for the free obedience to Christ's law of love proper to the children of God.

On the basis of this fundamental freedom, then, the possibilities of true Christian freedom are again opening out: freedom to worship God as our Father, not as an arbitrary lawgiver; as the God of Abraham, Isaac, and Jacob, the "Father of our Lord Jesus Christ," not as an abstract "Supreme Being"; freedom to find Christ where He reveals and gives Himself to us in the Church, no longer hidden from us by incomprehensible rites or by the fear that we shall misunderstand His Word; freedom to find and serve Christ in our neighbor, no longer held back by fear that we may lose our faith in coming closer to that neighbor; freedom to lay down our lives in service of our brethren and so to follow Christ through death to life; in short, freedom to "live and walk in the Spirit."

The role of the Church, therefore, is now clearly not so much to protect as to communicate—to communicate Christ's truth and life to her members and, through them, to all of human society. It is not so much to conserve as to grow—to "grow up in all things in Christ by doing the truth in love." It is not to keep its members safe, but to open out to them in all its urgency Christ's invitation to lose their lives in order to find them. It is not to protect itself from a hostile world, but to go out to proclaim the Good News in word and life and to make that Good News credible by the witness of Christian love.

It is in this new context, then, that all our present institutions, including the Catholic school system, must be examined.

11

CONCLUSIONS

In the present state of Catholic education, one of three general courses of action seems possible: to keep on as we are; to make an all-out attempt to secure whole or partial public support of our Catholic school system or to establish something like the shared-time plan; or to concentrate our efforts on the work of the renewal, caring for the formation of young Catholics in the framework of this wider objective.

To keep on as we are, struggling to support and extend the Catholic educational system by our own efforts, is clearly becoming less and less feasible. The evidence seems to indicate that this policy would mean educating fewer and fewer Catholics in proportion to the total number, while continuing to absorb a major part of the Church's personnel and material resources.

Before we decide to extend our efforts to secure whole or partial public support for our schools—perhaps by the method proposed in the "Junior G.I. Bill"—we should consider carefully what the effects would be if we secured this support. In the unlikely circumstance that total public support like that given to the public schools were secured, we should be committing ourselves to providing schools at the elementary and secondary level for all Catholic children. The

Church would be saddled with the burden of supervising the construction of more than double the number of schools it maintains at present; and of administering and staffing them. Not only would this mean a vastly increased burden of administration for bishops, diocesan boards, and pastors, but also, since there are not anywhere nearly enough religious teachers for our present needs, large numbers of lay teachers and lay administrators would have to be employed. Would a Catholic public still wedded to the concept that only religious can *really* provide a Catholic education welcome or support schools largely staffed by laity? No one knows the answer to this question; but obviously it must be asked.

In any event, such public support would mean that fewer and fewer Catholics would be teaching in the public schools, and that fewer and fewer Catholic citizens would be concerned with public-school problems. We should then have forfeited all possibility of influencing public education in the direction of a true humanism, more or less open to religion, and away from a narrow secularism entirely closed to it. This would leave the Protestant bodies who were not numerous enough to run their own schools to fight that battle alone.

At the same time the Catholic public would be cut off, even more than at present, from one of the major concerns of its fellow citizens, the welfare of the public schools. It is hard to imagine, in our own country, a complex of schools and school systems run by various religious bodies, with the public schools reduced to comparative unimportance, but even if this came about it seems fair to predict that the prevailing standards would still be set by the ethos of state education. Nor does it seem likely that such a complex would ultimately further true religious pluralism, but rather "vertical pluralism"—that is, a multiplicity of religious groups, each with its own life and its own subculture carried on alongside of, but not interpenetrating, those of other groups.

A successful effort to make the shared-time plan universal would relieve Catholic school systems of some major expenses and major personnel problems. But it would mean the abandonment of all attempt to work with members of other religious bodies toward inculcating in the public schools a true humanism, open to God even though not directly fostering belief in Him. The Christian churches themselves would be divided educationally—a situation which seems highly undesirable today, when we are called to work at every level toward the union of all those who believe in Christ. On this same level, the Christian churches would be further separated from Jewish groups rather than expanding the effort to find and explore common ground. And it would leave the Church responsible for providing instruction in the humanities for every Catholic child and adolescent.

These alternatives, and any possible variation or combination of them, would all mean, in short, that the Catholic Church in America would have to continue to spend itself on what is essentially an auxiliary service—auxiliary, that is, to its essential mission to build up the Body of Christ, to form hearers and doers of the Word, worshipers of the Father in Spirit and in truth.

The question at issue is not whether there should

be *any* Catholic schools. As I have suggested, there will always be a need for Catholic schools of various special kinds. The question is whether there should be a Catholic school *system,* maintained as part of the very structure of the Church. The question is not whether some of the Church's members should group together to provide a general education for some young Catholics under religious auspices, but whether the Church itself, through its basic diocesan and parochial structure, should remain in the field of general education.

The American Church has been in this field for so long and so extensively that to disengage itself now will be a very slow and difficult process. But since we must plan some course of action for the future, must we not ask ourselves whether such disengagement, carried on concurrently with an increasing engagement in the work of providing religious formation for all Catholics, would not ultimately prove the wisest course?

To be in the work of education at all today means providing a specialized professional service. It cannot be done on the side. If the Church itself, through its basic diocesan and parochial structure (and not merely some of its members, as with other auxiliary services), remains in the field of education as it exists in our country today, that work cannot help claiming a great part of the Church's total effort. It may be that in other countries, smaller and with a different educational tradition, the Church can, given state support, provide general education for all her young people and keep this auxiliary service in due proportion. But mass education in the United States cannot help being "big business." Can the Church in our country—with or without public support—continue to provide this auxiliary service and, at the same time, effectively pursue her first and true objective?

This question might legitimately have been asked even if the Council had not been convoked, and even if the Pope and the Council had not called for an ecumenical effort and a work of renewal. For in trying to provide a total Catholic education for as many of our young people as possible, we have been neglecting to provide anything like adequate *religious* formation for all those not in Catholic schools, and we have been neglecting the *religious* formation of adults. Yet to give religious *formation,* not only to children and young people but to all its members, is part of the Church's essential mission: "Go, make disciples of all nations"—a disciple being by definition a learner.

But the fact that such an effort and such a renewal are called for would seem to indicate beyond any doubt what the answer to the question must be. The Council, the ecumenical spirit, and the Catholic situation in the United States all point with increasing clarity to the role of the Church in America. In our pluralistic society, we are not called to continue or foster any kind of "vertical pluralism." The missionary nature of the Church itself indicates that this cannot be our aim. We are called, on the contrary, to witness to Christ and to His presence and activity in His Church on every level and in every aspect of our society.

And we can only carry out this work, first, by putting ourselves, and by helping to put one another, in as close contact as possible with the Christ who speaks to us and acts on us in His Word, in the sacrifice and sacraments of the Church, and then by putting ourselves in contact with our neighbor, sharing his interests and concerns, working with him for the welfare of all men. It is hard to see how, under present circumstances, the continuance or the extension of the Catholic school system can be anything but an obstacle to the pursuit of these aims.

ABOUT THE AUTHOR

MARY PERKINS RYAN has been associated with educators and educational reformers all her life. Her aunt, Mrs. Justine Ward, was the author of the Ward Method for teaching Gregorian Chant; her mother worked with Dr. T. E. Shields at Catholic University in his pioneering efforts to relate religion and the general curriculum, and also with the artist, Charles Woodbury, in his attempt to reform art education. Her husband, John Julian Ryan, professor of English at St. Anselm's College, Manchester, New Hampshire, is the author of several books, including *The Idea of a Catholic College.*

Mrs. Ryan began to write shortly after graduating from Manhattanville College. She is the author of eight books, including *Speaking of How to Pray, Key to the Psalms,* and *Perspectives for Renewal.* A frequent contributor to such periodicals as *Worship, Catholic Digest, The Commonweal, The Sign,* and *St. Joseph,* she also wrote an essay in the recent important symposium, *Modern Catechetics.*

Mrs. Ryan is the mother of five boys who have attended both Catholic and public schools. As her earlier *Beginning at Home* and *Mind the Baby* demonstrate, she has always emphasized the idea of parental responsibility in the problem of religious formation of children.

After attending the first Liturgical Week in Chicago in 1940, Mrs. Ryan became deeply involved in the liturgical movement and wrote the much-used pamphlet, "What is this 'Active Participation'?" A member of the board of directors of the National Liturgical Committee, she is also National Chairman of the Spiritual Development Committee of the National Council of Catholic Women.